The 5-Minute Spiritual Journal
for Christian Women

Interior and Cover Designer: Jane Archer
Art Producer: Megan Baggott
Editor: Brian Sweeting
Production Editor: Holland Baker
Production Manager: Jose Olivera

Illustrations by Jane Archer
Author photo courtesy of Carol Martinez/Revamped Media

Paperback ISBN: 978-1-63807-379-6
R0

5-MINUTE
SPIRITUAL
JOURNAL

for CHRISTIAN WOMEN

Inspiring Prompts to Reflect
and Connect with God

AMY AYALA

**ROCKRIDGE
PRESS**

TO THE ONE HOLDING THIS BOOK:

YOU ARE FEARFULLY AND WONDERFULLY MADE.

CONTENTS

Introduction   vi

How to Use This Journal   vii

JOURNAL ENTRIES   1

A Final Word   159

INTRODUCTION

Welcome to the *5-Minute Spiritual Journal for Christian Women*! I have been praying for you all the way through the making of this book, so I believe if you're reading this right now, then God desires to speak to your life and bring you deeper into relationship with Him!

I've always believed that the turning point for my life was when I not only began to read the Bible, but when I received His Word. I grew up as a church kid—I attended all the services, took all the right steps, and did what I thought made me a good Christian. However, it wasn't until He became my Savior on a personal level that everything changed.

When I was 19, Jesus began knocking on the door of my heart like never before, but this time was different. The knocks were louder, and I could no longer deny Him entry. I opened the door to my heart completely, and I could not help but surrender to His love. It was in this moment that I began my relationship with Him. My soul yearned to know Him more, so I began to pour myself into the study of scripture.

God showed me that He is faithful to His Word in Matthew 7:7 (NIV): "Ask and it will be given to you; seek and you will find; knock and the door will be opened to you."

I trust that if you're here, it is because you desire to know Jesus more. My prayer is that this journal will help you grow closer to Him and that His deep and unconditional love for you will be a daily blessing.

HOW TO USE THIS JOURNAL

The Bible is an invitation to come and know God more deeply and intimately. This invitation is before you as you start this book. This journal will bring you in contact with the Word of God to help you believe, receive, and respond to it daily. Think of this journal as the space where you meet with God. Even if five minutes is all you have, then give God your all.

Come to this journal every day with your Bible. You'll find that in every entry there is scripture, a devotional, space to respond, and a prayer to wrap things up. I also encourage you to pray before you start any entry. Ask God to be the one leading your time together; tell Him to speak to you and to give you a heart that'll receive His Word. You're here because you want to grow in your relationship with God and you desire to hear from Him. I want you to know that God also desires to speak to you now through His Word. It is in His Word that you will find the answers you have been looking for, the lasting peace you have been yearning for, and the life that you were destined to live. I pray this journal enriches your time in the Word!

Faith isn't the ability to believe long and far into the misty future. It's simply taking God at His word and taking the next step.

—JONI EARECKSON TADA

Journal
Entries

PERFECT PEACE

*You will keep in perfect peace those whose minds are
steadfast, because they trust in you.*

—ISAIAH 26:3 NIV

God makes His perfect peace available to those who trust in Him. This is the
key: to trust God with your today and tomorrow. No matter the circumstance
or the season, you can rest in Him. What worries or burdens have been taking
away your peace? Can you surrender them to God today?

_____

_____

_____

_____

_____

_____

_____

_____

_____

_____

_____

God, I ask that you keep me in perfect peace today. Amen.

THE COMPARISON TRAP

Wait and trust the Lord. Don't be upset when others get rich or when someone else's plans succeed. Don't get angry. Don't be upset; it only leads to trouble . . . It is better to have little and be right than to have much and be wrong.

—PSALM 37:7–8, 16 NCV

Comparison will kill your vision, steal joy, and lead to trouble. Please remember that when others succeed, it doesn't hinder your success. God has promised plans to help you prosper—plans that will give you a future and hope. Below, write to God about your desires for the future. Ask for wisdom to help you pursue and achieve your goals.

_____

_____

_____

_____

_____

_____

God, help me trust in Your timing.
Your ways are perfect. Amen.

LETTING GO

For I am convinced that . . . neither the present nor the future . . . will be able to separate us from the love of God that is in Christ Jesus our Lord.

—ROMANS 8:38–39 NIV

Paul references the present and future in this verse, but not the past. Dwelling on the past can bring up feelings of regret or shame, and it can even keep you from knowing God's love. God wants to free you from the chains of yesterday and bring you into freedom. Is there something from the past you want freedom from?

_____

_____

_____

_____

_____

_____

_____

_____

God, help me forgive myself and walk in freedom. Amen.

WONDERFULLY MADE

For you created my inmost being; you knit me together in my mother's womb. I praise you because I am fearfully and wonderfully made; your works are wonderful, I know that full well.

—PSALM 139:13–14 NIV

God has spoken powerful words of life over you. You have been wonderfully and fearfully made. You were created with and for a purpose. You are beautiful. The Bible speaks of the power of our words. According to Proverbs 18:21 (NIV), "The tongue has the power of life and death." The words and thoughts you have about yourself matter. What encouragements will you write to yourself about your worth as God's masterpiece?

_____

_____

_____

_____

_____

_____

_____

God, teach me to see myself how You see me. Amen.

A FATHER'S CARE

Protect me from harm; keep an eye on me as you would a child who is reflected in the twinkling of your eye. Yes, hide me within the shelter of your embrace, under your outstretched wings.

—PSALM 17:8 TPT

The Father truly does watch over you and care for you. You are His. To be dependent on Him does not make you weak; it makes you strong, because you have learned that He is your fortress and shelter. Life was meant to be lived with Him. Have you taken pride in being self-sufficient? List some thoughts about how you might let go of burdens and embrace God's ability to care for you.

_____

_____

_____

_____

_____

_____

*God, I pray that You will wrap me in Your presence today.
Stay with me and be my place of shelter. Amen.*

GOD'S STRENGTH

He gives strength to the weary and increases the power of the weak.

—ISAIAH 40:29 NIV

With the ups and downs of life, it is easy to feel powerless and out of control. This may lead you to want to give up. But God wants to strengthen your hands and feet for the tasks at hand. He wants to refresh your soul and to remind you that you are not alone. What do you need strength for today? Tell the Lord; He is faithful and will respond.

_____

_____

_____

_____

_____

_____

_____

*God, don't allow my feeling of powerlessness to keep me
from Your purposes. Strengthen my spirit and renew my mind
so that I may move forward confidently. Amen.*

GOD IS WITH YOU

Be strong and courageous. Do not be afraid or terrified because of them, for the Lord your God goes with you; he will never leave you nor forsake you.

—DEUTERONOMY 31:6 NIV

There may be situations in your life that cause you to feel powerless. Today's verse reminds you that God will never leave or forget you. Not only that, but He will empower you to be strong and courageous, even in the midst of your troubles. Write to ask God to reveal His comforting presence to you as you experience specific fears.

_____

_____

_____

_____

_____

_____

_____

_____

God, I let go of my fear today and hold on to Your promises instead. Amen.

NEW MERCY

Because of the Lord's great love we are not consumed, for his compassions never fail. They are new every morning; great is your faithfulness.

—LAMENTATIONS 3:22–23 NIV

There is a forever promise of mercy over your life. God's mercy and compassion never come to an end. Whether covering a sin from 10 years ago or 10 seconds ago, His forgiveness is available. Walk in the authority of this truth today: You are forgiven. You are free. You are His. Have you ever felt like a captive of your past? Have you struggled with accepting God's forgiveness? Write about your experiences.

_____

_____

_____

_____

_____

_____

_____

God, teach me to walk in Your forgiveness and set me free from the guilt of my past. Amen.

PRAY EXPECTANTLY

"Therefore I tell you, whatever you ask for in prayer, believe that you have received it, and it will be yours."

—MARK 11:24 NIV

Pray as if God has already acted. Believe as if the answer has already come. No matter how small or great your request is, approach Him full of faith and confidence. Believe and you will receive! Write your prayer requests in the space below, believing that God will answer.

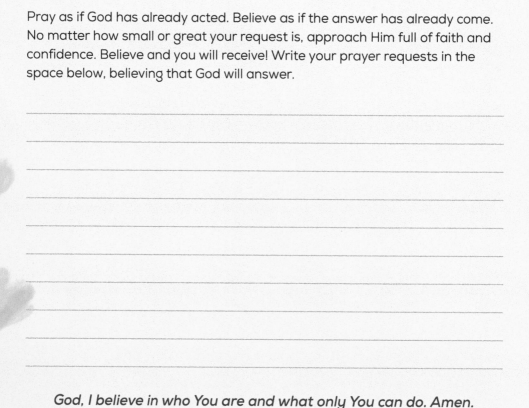

God, I believe in who You are and what only You can do. Amen.

YOU WILL NOT FALL

The Lord makes firm the steps of the one who delights in him; though he may stumble, he will not fall, for the Lord upholds him with his hand.

—PSALM 37:23-24 NIV

God is not surprised by mistakes, nor does He walk away when we stumble. God searches and examines the heart, because the intentions of your heart are far more important to God than your mistakes. Every day, invite God to transform you from the inside out. Have you ever felt the need to perform well or to be perfect for God? Consider how that mentality might affect your relationship with God versus approaching Him more vulnerably.

God, thank You for being steadfast even though I make mistakes. You are still here, and You hold me together. Amen.

GOD ANSWERS

At the very moment I called out to you, you answered me!
You strengthened me deep within my soul and breathed
fresh courage into me.

—PSALM 138:3 TPT

God not only hears you, but He responds to you. All you need to do is call out to Him. What is it that you need today? Is it peace? Or maybe you're in need of strength to make it through another day. Come to God today. He desires for you to know Him as a loving Father who is a proven help in times of trouble. Take some time to share your prayer request with God. Speak to Him and He will answer.

_____

_____

_____

_____

_____

_____

_____

_____

God, tune into my prayer and listen to the cries of my heart. Amen.

WONDERFUL WORKS

I will worship you, Yahweh, with extended hands as my whole heart erupts with praise! I will tell everyone everywhere about your wonderful works!

—PSALM 9:1 TPT

We can praise God when we speak about His wonderful works! As you speak about His wonders, joy fills your heart and reminds you that He is the God of miracles. Not only that, but everyone around you will be encouraged by what God has done in your life. Make a list of the wonderful things—big and small—that God has done in your life.

_____

_____

_____

_____

_____

_____

_____

God, I praise You for all Your wonderful works! You are good.
Thank You for Your care over me. I love You, Lord. Amen.

THROUGH IT ALL

"When you pass through the deep, stormy sea, you can count on me to be there with you. When you pass through raging rivers, You will not drown. When you walk through persecution like fiery flames, you will not be burned; the flames will not harm you."

—ISAIAH 43:2 TPT

Friend, you can count on God! Maybe people have let you down in the past. They walked away when you needed them the most. God wants you to know that He is not like them. He will never leave you and He will never forsake you. His love is loyal: He will stick with you through it all. Describe a time when trusting God was difficult for you because of what people have done to you in the past.

_____

_____

_____

_____

_____

_____

*God, I will count on You through this trial. No matter what may come,
I know that I am safe with You by my side. I trust in You. Amen.*

PROMISE OF PEACE

"Even if the mountains were to crumble and the hills disappear, my heart of steadfast, faithful love will never leave you, and my covenant of peace with you will never be shaken," says Yahweh, whose love and compassion will never give up on you.

—ISAIAH 54:10 TPT

Everything may crumble around you; trouble may knock on your door, and the world may waste away. Whatever happens, God refuses to leave you. In fact, even amidst chaos and trouble, His peace is available to you. He has promised this, and He never goes back on His Word. How does it feel to know that God is with you, even here?

_____

_____

_____

_____

_____

God, even in the most difficult seasons of my life,
thank You for never walking away. Amen.

THE SECRET

I know what it means to lack, and I know what it means to experience overwhelming abundance. For I'm trained in the secret of overcoming all things, whether in fullness or in hunger. And I find that the strength of Christ's explosive power infuses me to conquer every difficulty.

—PHILIPPIANS 4:12–13 TPT

When your source of strength is Christ, then absolutely nothing can break you. His strength is in constant supply, and everything you need is in Him. You were never created to do life alone or to carry burdens on your shoulders. Jesus is with you: I encourage you to lean on Him. He is your place of strength. Have you been trying to do it all on your own instead of leaning on Jesus? What burdens can you give to Him today?

_____

_____

_____

_____

_____

_____

God, supply me with the strength I need. Teach me to lean not on myself but on You. Amen.

MAY HIS FAVOR BE WITH YOU

May the favor of the Lord our God rest on us; establish the work of our hands for us—yes, establish the work of our hands.

—PSALM 90:17 NIV

There is power in praying, "God, use my life." The person who makes themselves available to the Lord will be used greatly. Allow the Lord to lead you, and He will establish you. You will experience a favor you have never known before. Things you never imagined possible will happen for you. Would you allow yourself to be a vessel for His use? How could you glorify God through your work?

_____

_____

_____

_____

_____

_____

_____

God, establish the work of my hands. Whatever it is You lead me to do, may I bring glory to Your name. May there be less of me and more of You. God, use my life! Amen.

DON'T LOSE HEART

Therefore we do not lose heart. Though outwardly we are wasting away, yet inwardly we are being renewed day by day.

—2 CORINTHIANS 4:16 NIV

We are often so quick to ask God, "Why are you doing this *to* me?" instead of, "What are you trying to do *in* me?" God is concerned with growing you in all aspects of life. The experiences of life lead us to this growth. So, don't lose heart. Even while you're going through struggles, God is renewing you and doing beautiful work in you. What is something that God has taught you through experiences or seasons in your life?

_____

_____

_____

_____

_____

_____

God, keep me from being distracted by what is going on around me so I can focus on what You're doing in me. Amen.

LIVING EMPOWERED

For the Spirit God gave us does not make us timid, but gives us power, love and self-discipline.

—2 TIMOTHY 1:7 NIV

God did not design you to be controlled by fear but to be free and limitless by His Spirit. As His child, you can walk this life empowered, knowing that the Holy Spirit lives within you. Has fear ever kept you from experiencing life? Write about it, inviting the Holy Spirit into every aspect of your life.

_____

_____

_____

_____

_____

_____

_____

_____

_____

_____

Father God, fill me with Your spirit so that I can know the gift of freedom. Amen.

LIVE WISELY

Be very careful, then, how you live—not as unwise but as wise, making the most of every opportunity, because the days are evil.

—EPHESIANS 5:15–16 NIV

Do you make wise decisions? Who do you spend your time with? How are you making the most of your day? These are questions you should ask yourself every single day. Every day is filled with opportunities: Ask God for wisdom and discernment so you can seize them. Every day counts and every decision matters, so ask God to lead you. Consider how you can spend your time wisely and what actions you can take to make the most of your days.

_____

_____

_____

_____

_____

_____

_____

_____

God, I hand this day over to You. Lead me and give me Your wisdom. Amen.

INSIDE OUT

Fix your attention on God. You'll be changed from the inside out.

—ROMANS 12:2 MSG

There will always be external things trying to steal your attention away from God, from work projects to interpersonal challenges. You can choose to focus first on keeping God at the center of your heart, to be molded by Him and changed from the inside out. What besides God has gotten your attention lately? How has this affected your inner spiritual life?

_____

_____

_____

_____

_____

_____

_____

_____

God, help me avoid looking to my right or left, but straight at You. Keep me focused on You. Amen.

GOD'S MASTERPIECE

For we are God's handiwork, created in Christ Jesus to do good works, which God prepared in advance for us to do.

—EPHESIANS 2:10 NIV

Right now, maybe your life feels like a bunch of pieces that don't make sense and don't exactly fit together. God knows how to bring all the abstract pieces together. He knows how to give beauty for ashes. You are God's masterpiece, and each and every part of you is beautiful and unique. Good things await you because you are called to radiate God's goodness. How does this verse encourage you today?

_____

_____

_____

_____

_____

_____

_____

_____

_____

God, I trust You are making something beautiful out of the pieces of my life. Glorify Yourself through me. Amen.

NEW MERCY, NEW OPPORTUNITY

*This is the very day of the Lord that bring gladness and joy,
filling our hearts with glee.*

—PSALM 118:24 TPT

God's mercies are made new every single morning. This mercy brings hope
and allows you to choose joy. Yesterday might've been heavy, tiring, or crush-
ing. Don't allow it to linger—today is a new day filled with new opportunity, and
you have God's permission to rejoice in it and to rejoice in Him. Describe how it
makes you feel to know that you have a fresh start with God today.

_____

_____

_____

_____

_____

_____

_____

_____

*God, thank You for this new day, thank You for new
opportunities, and thank You for Your mercy. Amen.*

PARTNER WITH GOD

For, "Everyone who calls on the name of the Lord will be saved."

—ROMANS 10:13 NIV

There are no lost causes for God. Whoever calls on Him shall be saved. It doesn't matter what you've been through, His love triumphs over all and His blood covers all. God wants you to partner with Him and believe in salvation for your friends and family. Do you have any loved ones you can be sharing Jesus with? Write their names and a prayer over them.

_____

_____

_____

_____

_____

_____

_____

_____

God, I believe that You can save my friends and family. I ask that You touch their lives so they can experience Your love. Amen.

FREEDOM IN TRUTH

"Then you will know the truth, and the truth will set you free."

—JOHN 8:32 NIV

The truth of God's Word brings freedom. It breaks the chains of lies that the enemy wants you to believe. Every day, seek to discover His truth, which is far more precious than gold. Ask that His truth will illuminate your path through what holds you back today, whether it's fear of failure or self-doubt.

_____

_____

_____

_____

_____

_____

_____

_____

_____

*God, show me the way and show me Your truth so
I can be led by it. Amen.*

WITNESS OF THE LIGHT

He came as a witness to testify concerning that light, so that through him all might believe.

—JOHN 1:7 NIV

It's wonderful to think that God has put His love on display through your life. Through you and your testimony, many will come to believe. Just as He used John the Baptist, so will He use you. How can you share the love of God with those around you? Write down some ideas.

_____

_____

_____

_____

_____

_____

_____

_____

_____

_____

*God, use my life so that through me, many
will come to know You. Amen.*

GIFT OF SALVATION

For the wages of sin is death, but the gift of God is eternal life in Christ Jesus our Lord.

—ROMANS 6:23 NIV

God has removed the guilty verdict over your life and has called you innocent. All sins of the past, present, and future have been paid for by Jesus. He has made sinners into sons and daughters. Today, rejoice as you accept this beautiful gift from God. Take some time in this space to thank God for the gift of salvation.

_____

_____

_____

_____

_____

_____

_____

_____

*God, thank You for Your gift of salvation. Thank You for
Your unconditional love for me. Amen.*

LIVING TO MAKE HIM KNOWN

*I will perpetuate your memory through all generations;
therefore the nations will praise you for ever and ever.*

—PSALM 45:17 NIV

The psalmist speaks about living to make God known. The goal of believers should be the same: magnifying God through our lives. The focus must be His glory, not ours, so that others may know Him, whether we're sharing personal testimony of His good works or offering to pray for a troubled friend or serving those around us. Write some ways you can make God known to those around you in your daily life.

_____

_____

_____

_____

_____

_____

_____

_____

_____

*God, use my life to magnify Your name and
to make You known. Amen.*

EVERYTHING YOU NEED

The Lord gives strength to his people; the Lord blesses his people with peace.

—PSALM 29:11 NIV

Everything you need is found in the Lord. He will supply you with the strength you need to face the day in front of you. He will fill you with peace that surpasses all understanding. What do you need from the Lord today? In the space below, ask Him for it with faith.

_____

_____

_____

_____

_____

_____

_____

_____

_____

God, would You bless me today with Your peace and with all that I will need? Amen.

PUT YOUR TRUST IN GOD

In God I trust and am not afraid. What can man do to me?

—PSALM 56:11 NIV

Those who have placed their trust in God will live their lives unafraid. People can harm you and try to break you, but God will sustain you through it all. His plans for your life are good and His plans always prevail. Live unafraid in the care of the Father. Has the decision to trust God ever helped you overcome? Write about it below, reminding yourself of the power of trusting God.

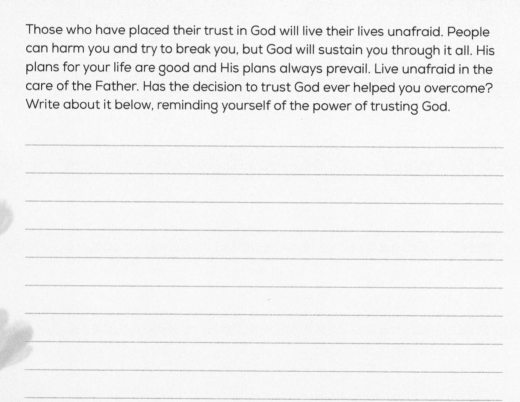

*God, free me from my fears, because I have
placed my trust in You. Amen.*

SHE WHO BELIEVES

"Blessed is she who has believed that the Lord would fulfill his promises to her!"

—LUKE 1:45 NIV

For every word God has spoken, there is promised fulfillment. When you're in the gap between the promise and the fulfillment, believe and have faith that God will do what He has said. Have you struggled to believe God's promises for your life? Write about your experiences. Remind yourself to pray and allow this to encourage your heart today.

_____

_____

_____

_____

_____

_____

_____

God, I believe in who You are and all that You can do.
Fill my heart with more faith today. Amen.

LOVE WISDOM

The fear of the Lord is the beginning of knowledge, but fools despise wisdom and instruction.

—PROVERBS 1:7 NIV

The Lord's instruction and correction come from a place of love for His children. The child who receives them is made wise by God. God desires for you to experience growth in every area of your life. Lend your ear to the Father's instruction. Do you ask the Lord for wisdom? Do you want to experience growth in any area of your life? Pray to God and write about the steps you need to take to grow.

_____

_____

_____

_____

_____

_____

_____

_____

God, teach me and correct me. Grace me
with more wisdom. Amen.

CONSIDER JOY

Consider it pure joy, my brothers and sisters, whenever you face trials of many kinds, because you know that the testing of your faith produces perseverance.

—JAMES 1:2-3 NIV

Trials not only test your faith, but they also grow your faith. Trials make you unshakable and unmovable through trusting God to persevere. The Lord becomes your rock when you look to Him in every season. What you are facing is not meaningless; God has divine purpose behind it. Take heart today, allow God to lead you in the process, and let the Lord be your strength. What trials are you facing? Take some time to ask God to show you the joy that is still available.

_____

_____

_____

_____

_____

_____

God, give me Your gift of joy today and allow me to experience it. Amen.

YOU AND YOUR FAMILY

They replied, "Believe in the Lord Jesus, and you will be saved—you and your household."

—ACTS 16:31 NIV

God has plans for you in regard to your family. You can believe for salvation for you and your household. God has strategically placed you to be a light and a direct reflection of His love. Don't lose hope. Continue praying for, loving, and serving them. Write a prayer for the salvation of your family in the space below. Write down their names and remember this day.

_____

_____

_____

_____

_____

_____

_____

_____

God, I believe for salvation for me and my household.
My family belongs to You. Amen.

CHARGED WITH FAITH

"Truly I tell you, if anyone says to this mountain, 'Go, throw yourself into the sea,' and does not doubt in their heart but believes that what they say will happen, it will be done for them."

—MARK 11:23 NIV

Every word you pray must be charged with faith. It's not enough to pray empty words with a doubtful heart. You are praying to a mighty God who wants to do mighty works through you. Consider what seems the most impossible need or desire of your heart. Then, write it in a prayer to God, believing with all your heart that it will be done.

_____

_____

_____

_____

_____

_____

God, remove any traces of doubt that are within me, so that I can believe with all of my heart in what You can do. Amen.

SHOW ME THE WAY

Your word is a lamp for my feet, a light on my path.

—PSALM 119:105 NIV

If you've been asking God to speak to you, you can hear Him today through His Word. His Word will give you direction and discernment. Allow His words to guide you, lead you, and be a lamp for your feet. Have you been spending time in the Word of God? Take a few moments with God right now and write your thoughts to Him. Ask Him to speak to you and give you wisdom and guidance.

_____

_____

_____

_____

_____

_____

_____

_____

_____

God, reveal to me Your Word. May it light my way and lead me to where You need me to be. Amen.

KEEP YOUR CONFIDENCE

So do not throw away your confidence; it will be richly rewarded.

—HEBREWS 10:35 NIV

Don't allow your current situation to take away your confidence in God. Continue trusting in who He is. Remember, your confidence is not in what *you* can do but in what *He* can do. He is greater than any challenge that you face. With God on your side, victory is sure. Write about the greatness of God. Remind your heart and mind about who He is.

_____

_____

_____

_____

_____

_____

_____

_____

*God, You are my rock. You are my confidence. I know You won't
let me down, so I will continue looking to You. Amen.*

7

EXCEEDINGLY ABUNDANT

Now to him who is able to do immeasurably more than all we ask or imagine, according to his power that is at work within us.

—EPHESIANS 3:20 NIV

He is not a God of lack. He is a God of abundance. He is the God of the impossible. He is able to do more than your mind can even imagine. It's important to remember who it is you pray to. He is able to exceed all of your expectations! Have you struggled with unmet expectations? If so, has this hindered your prayers? What can you do to expand your expectations and let God be in control?

_____

_____

_____

_____

_____

_____

_____

God, You know the desires of my heart. Give me faith to believe in who You are and what You can do. I believe that You are a God of abundance, so allow me to see that in my life. Amen.

THE GIFT OF PEACE

"Peace I leave with you; my peace I give you. I do not give to you as the world gives. Do not let your hearts be troubled and do not be afraid."

—JOHN 14:27 NIV

The peace God has for you is not circumstantial; it is constant. It surpasses all understanding. The peace the world offers is short lived, but God's peace lasts forever. This is a gift from the Father to His children. You can be surrounded by trouble and still be under the protection of God. Take a moment to reflect and write about who or what you've been running to for peace besides God. How might you better take comfort in Him?

_____

_____

_____

_____

_____

_____

*God, I want the peace that comes from You. I will
no longer try to find it in the world or for myself, but
You will be my source. Amen.*

RETURN TO THE FATHER

"Therefore tell the people: This is what the Lord Almighty says: 'Return to me,' declares the Lord Almighty, 'and I will return to you,' says the Lord Almighty."

—ZECHARIAH 1:3 NIV

It doesn't matter how far away from God you feel. God's love for you is greater than anything. He is waiting with arms wide open for you. God is not finished with you. The Father is calling you to return and come back into His care. Have any mistakes kept you in a place of guilt or shame? What are you doing to work through those feelings? Approach God today and receive His forgiveness and unconditional love. He is waiting for you.

_____

_____

_____

_____

_____

_____

_____

_____

*God, forgive and restore me. Wash me clean and
make me new. In Jesus' name, amen.*

GOD STANDS FOREVER

"The grass withers and the flowers fall, but the word of our God endures forever."

—ISAIAH 40:8 NIV

Everything here on earth comes to an end. But God is forever. His Word is forever. So often we treasure the temporary over the eternal. Priorities will reveal what you value most. Take a moment to write about what you have been giving importance in your life. Does it carry eternal value? How can you further prioritize God in your life?

_____

_____

_____

_____

_____

_____

_____

_____

God, teach me to value the eternal more than the temporary. Teach me to stand on the truth of Your Word and to love it. Amen.

ACKNOWLEDGE GOD

Trust in the Lord with all your heart and lean not on your own understanding; in all your ways submit to him, and he will make your paths straight.

—PROVERBS 3:5–6 NIV

Often our prayers can seem like we're giving advice to God rather than asking God for guidance. Let's be real: We often think that we know best. But we should acknowledge God's power and that He is in control. He requests our absolute trust in Him to take us where we need to be, when we need to be there. Have you been trying to direct God, or are you letting Him lead you? How might you better live in acknowledgment of God at the wheel?

_____

_____

_____

_____

_____

_____

_____

_____

God, I trust in you and your timing. Guide and lead me in all my ways. Let Your will be done, not mine. Amen.

HE KNOWS

"For I know the plans I have for you," declares the Lord,
"plans to prosper you and not to harm you, plans to give
you hope and a future."

—JEREMIAH 29:11 NIV

God is saying to you today, "I know." Allow these words to wash over you and fill you with peace. As you face questions about the future, remember that nothing that happens will surprise God. God already knows and He is not confused about how or when to do it. The plans He has for you will bring good, and they will give you hope. Focus on the present moment you are in, and allow God to take care of the future. Write about some of your dreams and goals and surrender them to God.

_____

_____

_____

_____

_____

_____

God, my future is in Your hands. Remove any
traces of anxiety within me, for I trust You
with my today and tomorrow. Amen.

FRUITS OF THE SPIRIT

But the fruit of the Spirit is love, joy, peace, forbearance, kindness, goodness, faithfulness, gentleness and self-control. Against such things there is no law.

—GALATIANS 5:22–23 NIV

All the fruits of the Spirit are available to you. Some might feel more difficult to employ than others, but the Holy Spirit wants to empower you with them. Every single one of these fruits can be life changing. Today, choose a couple of the fruits from this verse, and ask the Spirit for moments to practice and grow in them with His help.

_____

_____

_____

_____

_____

_____

_____

God, I want to bear more of Your fruits. Help me in my weakness and help me grow. Amen.

SO LOVED

For God so loved the world that he gave his one and only Son, that whoever believes in him shall not perish but have eternal life.

—JOHN 3:16 NIV

May this beautiful reminder wash over you today. YOU are so loved by God! His love came in and changed everything. This is the reason for the hope within you. This is why you can experience joy today. It is all because of Jesus. In the space below, take some time to thank Him for His sacrifice on the cross.

_____

_____

_____

_____

_____

_____

_____

_____

_____

_____

Jesus, thank You for saving me from my sin.
I love You, Lord. Amen.

LEAD ME

For the Lord gives wisdom; from his mouth come knowledge and understanding.

—PROVERBS 2:6 NIV

If you find yourself in need of direction, ask God to lead you. If you're confused about what decision to make, ask God for counsel. The one who asks will receive. He will lead you with His knowledge and understanding. The answer you have been looking for is found in Him. Take some time to share your life with God and ask Him to lead you.

_____

_____

_____

_____

_____

_____

_____

_____

God, lead me with Your words of wisdom.
Give me understanding. Amen.

LOVE IS THE WAY

"By this everyone will know that you are my disciples, if you love one another."

—JOHN 13:35 NIV

Love is the evidence of God. How we love others matters. God will use love as the path for everyone to know who He is! God is inviting you to be a reflection of Him and the love He has for everyone. How can you make yourself available to God? Is it by feeding someone or being by their side when they're in pain? How can you better love those around you?

_____

_____

_____

_____

_____

_____

_____

_____

_____

God, help me love others the way You love me. Amen.

FOLLOW THE LEADER

"Whoever serves me must follow me; and where I am, my servant also will be. My Father will honor the one who serves me."

—JOHN 12:26 NIV

Every day, there is a decision of surrender. There is the choice of whether or not to follow Jesus. The desire of our hearts as His children is to be where He is, to go where He leads, and to follow all He says. God will honor those who live this way. Reflect on your life: Have you been leading or following Jesus? In what ways do you need to further surrender to Him?

_____

_____

_____

_____

_____

_____

_____

_____

God, today I choose to follow You and to surrender to all of Your ways. Amen.

TALK IS CHEAP

All hard work brings a profit, but mere talk leads only to poverty.

—PROVERBS 14:23 NIV

Action must back up our words. The Bible instructs us to make the most of every opportunity (Ephesians 5:16). Every day that God gives us is a new opportunity to work hard and progress by small or big steps. God sees the way that you work, if you're being diligent and faithful. He desires to bless you and honor you. Today is an opportunity to achieve goals and step closer to the dreams that God has placed within you. What actions can you take today to make the most of the opportunities God has provided?

_____

_____

_____

_____

_____

_____

_____

_____

God, thank You for a new day and an opportunity to work.
May You be glorified in all that I do. Amen.

KEEP ON

So let's keep on giving our thanks to God, for he is so good!
His constant, tender love lasts forever!

—PSALM 118:29 TPT

In the midst of the challenges and the heartache, "keep on" giving thanks to God! He is always worthy and deserving. Maintain a posture of praise to God, elevate Him over your troubles, and allow His goodness to wash over you. Don't allow any circumstance to muzzle your praise. On the following lines, list 10 reasons you are thankful to God today.

_____

_____

_____

_____

_____

_____

_____

_____

God, You are worthy of all praise!
You are good, always good. Amen.

IN HIS HANDS

I'm desperate, Lord! I throw myself upon you, for you alone are my God! My life, my every moment, my destiny—it's all in your hands.

—PSALM 31:14–15 TPT

God wants to interrupt the worry that you have been feeling about your future and bring you peace. Let this verse wash over you today and give you rest. Your life is in God's hands, where you are safe and taken care of. Cast your cares on Him, and share with Him your worries, because there is freedom in letting go.

_____

_____

_____

_____

_____

_____

_____

God, I trust You with my life, my every moment, and my destiny. I let go of all my worries, and I ask that Your peace come over me. Amen.

WORDS OF TRUTH

"Sanctify them by the truth; your word is truth."

—JOHN 17:17 NIV

Live in the truth by living in the Word of God. Immerse yourself in the Word and allow it to lead, guide, and enlighten all your ways. When you come to the Word, pray that there would be less of you and more of Him. Come with humility and a teachable heart that can receive all that God has for you. Think about who or what shapes your thoughts. Have you gone to the Word to receive truth?

God, show me Your truth so that I may live by it. Amen.

OPEN THE DOOR

"Here I am! I stand at the door and knock. If anyone hears my voice and opens the door, I will come in and eat with that person, and they with me."

Jesus is never intrusive and will never be an unwanted guest. His love patiently waits for you to open the door and let Him in. Jesus desires a real and intimate relationship with you. Friend, you hold the key to step into deeper communion with Him. Do you feel that there are areas in your life that you have kept Jesus out of? If so, why have you left Him out?

_____

_____

_____

_____

_____

_____

_____

God, I open myself to You, and I want to know You more. Make Your home in my heart. Amen.

THE LORD SAID

Now the Lord said to Abram, "Go from your country and your kindred and your father's house to the land that I will show you."

The most encouraging words in this verse are, "the Lord said." The Lord instructed Abram to go to an unknown land, and Abram responded in obedience. In the face of a new challenge, Abram moved forward, full of faith, into the unknown, because "the Lord said." When you move with God, you leave no room for fear to take hold of you. Listen to what God is leading you to do, and He will supply you with the faith you need. Has God been placing any projects or dreams in your heart? Has fear of the unknown kept you from moving forward?

_____

_____

_____

_____

_____

_____

God, I will trust all that You say. I will move at Your word with an obedient heart. Rid me of any fear that may want to hold me back. Amen.

REASON FOR HOPE

But in your hearts revere Christ as Lord. Always be prepared to give an answer to everyone who asks you to give the reason for the hope that you have. But do this with gentleness and respect.

—1 PETER 3:15 NIV

Knowing the Lord happens in the secret place. It happens in the ordinary moments where His presence meets you, and where He sanctifies and transforms you from the inside out. People may take note of the changes within you, and you will have the opportunity to share about your relationship with God. You will be prepared to give reason for your hope because you know Him. Do you have a special experience you have shared with the Lord? How can your relationship with God inspire others?

_____

_____

_____

_____

_____

Father God, grant me the opportunity to share with others about Your love. Reach me so that I may reach others. Amen.

TRUST GOD'S TIMING

But do not forget this one thing, dear friends: With the Lord a day is like a thousand years, and a thousand years are like a day. The Lord is not slow in keeping his promise, as some understand slowness. Instead he is patient with you, not wanting anyone to perish, but everyone to come to repentance.

—2 PETER 3:8–9 NIV

Be encouraged today that God knows the right time. He is never too early or too late. The seasons of waiting are serving a great purpose within you. God is concerned not only with the fulfillment of a promise but also with who you become in the process. God is in control. He knows what He is doing in and around you. What have you been waiting for God to do or to answer? Ask Him for patience in the wait and surrender control to Him.

*God, teach me to be patient and to wait on Your timing.
Let it be Your will and not my own. Amen.*

WORTHY OF OUR CALLING

As a prisoner for the Lord, then, I urge you to live a life worthy of the calling you have received.

—EPHESIANS 4:1 NIV

Knowing that you have been called and set apart by God will change the way that you walk. You have been created to live an extraordinary life that points to His redemptive power. Whatever you do, do it for the glory of God. With each and every breath, and with each moment that God gives, seek to glorify God through your actions. How does knowing that we are meant to live in a way that is worthy of our calling change the way you view your daily walk?

_____

_____

_____

_____

_____

_____

_____

_____

God, give me the strength and courage to live in a way that is worthy of You. Use my life to bring glory to Your name. Amen.

REDEMPTION IN JESUS

In him we have redemption through his blood, the forgiveness of sins, in accordance with the riches of God's grace.

—EPHESIANS 1:7 NIV

Redemption can't be earned. It is not won by good behavior or by being a good person. Redemption is a gift that is available because of what Jesus did on the cross. This brings hope to a believer. We are saved not by striving but by believing in Jesus. He is the perfect sacrifice for imperfect sinners like you and me. If your conscience ever wants to bring shame and guilt upon you, remember that you have been redeemed and completely forgiven by Jesus! Do you have confidence in His forgiveness? How does this passage help you?

God, I let go of any shame or guilt that has been over me, and I welcome Your forgiveness today. Amen.

DWELL WITHIN ME

You, however, are not in the realm of the flesh but are in the realm of the Spirit, if indeed the Spirit of God lives in you. And if anyone does not have the Spirit of Christ, they do not belong to Christ.

—ROMANS 8:9 NIV

What a powerful verse! Let this truth fill you today: The Spirit of God lives within you! The same Spirit that resurrected Jesus from the dead resides within you. Be encouraged that you are not fighting alone. The Holy Spirit is with you. Have you been going through life trying to do everything on your own? How can you lean on the Spirit today?

_____

_____

_____

_____

_____

_____

_____

Holy Spirit, dwell within me so that I may experience Your life-giving power. Amen.

SPIRIT LED

So I say, walk by the Spirit, and you will not gratify the desires of the flesh.

—GALATIANS 5:16 NIV

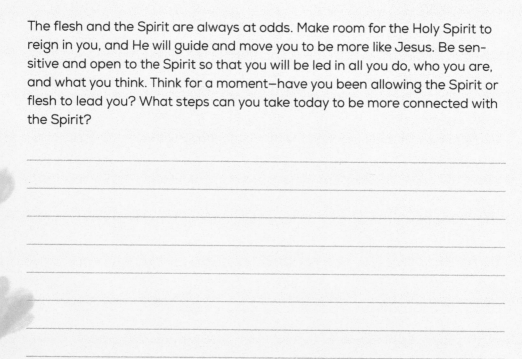

The flesh and the Spirit are always at odds. Make room for the Holy Spirit to reign in you, and He will guide and move you to be more like Jesus. Be sensitive and open to the Spirit so that you will be led in all you do, who you are, and what you think. Think for a moment—have you been allowing the Spirit or flesh to lead you? What steps can you take today to be more connected with the Spirit?

_____

_____

_____

_____

_____

_____

_____

_____

Father, teach me to walk by the Spirit and to let go of sin and all that entices the flesh. Help me in my weakness and lead me to live more like You. Amen.

THROUGH HIM AND FOR HIM

For in him all things were created: things in heaven and on earth, visible and invisible, whether thrones or powers or rulers or authorities; all things have been created through him and for him.

—COLOSSIANS 1:16 NIV

You were designed to radiate the glory of God. You were created through Him and for Him. In all you do today, do it for the glory and exaltation of God. How can you bring glory to God in your daily life?

_____

_____

_____

_____

_____

_____

_____

_____

God, may all I do be for Your glory. Amen.

ENTHRONED

Since, then, you have been raised with Christ, set your hearts on things above, where Christ is, seated at the right hand of God. Set your minds on things above, not on earthly things.

—COLOSSIANS 3:1–2 NIV

This is the vision of heaven for your life: Just as Jesus is enthroned and highly exalted in heaven, allow Him to be enthroned in your heart. What have you been pursuing, the temporary or the eternal? Make the passion and pursuit of your heart be for the eternal.

_____

_____

_____

_____

_____

_____

_____

_____

Father, teach me to value the eternal and help me keep my heart and mind there. Amen.

SUBMIT TO GOD

Submit yourselves, then, to God. Resist the devil, and he will flee from you.

—JAMES 4:7 NIV

Stand against the devil by submitting to God. This is how you will find strength to withstand his plots and schemes against you. Come under God's Word, and mold your life by it. Allow God to be the Lord of your life, and believe in the promise that the enemy will flee from you. Have you been fighting a spiritual battle lately? What does submission to God look like for you?

_____

_____

_____

_____

_____

_____

_____

God, come and be the Lord over my life. I surrender completely to Your will and ways. Amen.

GOOD SHEPHERD

"I am the good shepherd. The good shepherd lays down his life for the sheep."

—JOHN 10:11 NIV

Jesus gave His life so that we may have eternal life. He is the good shepherd who is willing to go anywhere and do anything for the sake of His sheep. This includes you; His eyes are ever on you. Come under the care of the Shepherd. His wish is to protect you, lead you, and watch over you. Do you try to do life on your own and avoid fully coming under the care of Jesus? What might you do to let God be your shepherd?

_____

_____

_____

_____

_____

_____

_____

*Jesus, You are my shepherd and I trust
You to lead and guide me. Amen.*

NEVER TOO FAR GONE

"But everyone my Father has given to me, they will come. And all who come to me, I will embrace and will never turn them away."

—JOHN 6:37 TPT

This is a beautiful reminder from Jesus. He will never turn you away. If you've ever felt that you're too far gone and that you can't come to God because of too many mistakes, may you know today that you are embraced, not rejected, by God. God loves you and it is not too late to come to Him. In fact, He's been waiting for you. Have you ever struggled with shame? Has that kept you from seeking God? How will you turn to Him?

God, thank You for never giving up on me and showing me the greatness of Your love. Amen.

LIVE FOR CHRIST

"He himself bore our sins" in his body on the cross, that we might die to sins and live for righteousness. "By his wounds you have been healed."

—1 PETER 2:24 NIV

Jesus gave His life so that sin would no longer separate us from Him, as He reigns in our hearts as Savior. He provided the way to renewal, life, and living in right relationship with Him. May the reality of what Jesus did burn brightly within you and fill you with passion to live for Him. Take some time today to thank Him for removing the debt and making a way.

_____

_____

_____

_____

_____

_____

_____

God, thank You for the gift of salvation in Your Son, who died for my sin so that I can live with You forever. Amen.

THE HELPER

In the same way, the Spirit helps us in our weakness. We do not know what we ought to pray for, but the Spirit himself intercedes for us through wordless groans.

—ROMANS 8:26 NIV

Has it ever been hard to pray when you're going through difficulties? I encourage you not to give up and to lean on the Spirit's help in prayer. Jesus promised He would leave us the Helper, the Holy Spirit. That means the Spirit is available not only to help you in your weakness but also to intercede on your behalf. Today, even if you're feeling weak, come anyway. Ask the Holy Spirit to help you. In faith, begin writing your prayer, and lean on the Spirit to fill in the gaps.

_____

_____

_____

_____

_____

_____

_____

_____

Holy Spirit, come and fill me. Help me in my weakness. I need You. Amen.

HEART CHECK

Do not love the world or anything in the world. If anyone loves the world, love for the Father is not in them.

—1 JOHN 2:15 NIV

Take some time to think about what holds the attention and affections of your heart. Have you been more focused on the creation rather than the Creator? What God wants to give you far exceeds what can be gained with money or influence. Focus on the eternal and pursue it passionately. If you've been feeling an emptiness within you, know that the satisfaction your soul has been looking for can only be found in God.

God, keep my eyes focused on You and the eternal gifts You have to offer. Teach me to love You more and more. Amen.

USE YOUR GIFTS

We have different gifts, according to the grace given to each of us.

—ROMANS 12:6 NIV

God made you with uniquely beautiful gifts that cannot be duplicated by anyone else. He gave these gifts to you so that you may use them to glorify Him and bless others. God desires that you would value your gifts and calling. Today, embrace your gifts, and ask God to reveal more of them so you can use them to serve. Have you ever shied away from your gifts because of fear? How can your gifts serve others?

_____

_____

_____

_____

_____

_____

_____

_____

_____

God, thank You for creating me with gifts. Reveal them to me and teach me how to use them for Your glory. Amen.

BE PRUDENT

The simple believe anything, but the prudent give thought to their steps.

—PROVERBS 14:15 NIV

Get your truth from the source. John 17:17 (NIV) says, "Sanctify them by the truth; your word is truth." The Word of God must serve as a compass to lead you to all truth and give you discernment in all your ways. It will help you distinguish what is right from wrong. Don't allow yourself to be shifted and pulled by different ideologies, opinions, or people, but be established by the truth of the Word. Think for a moment about your sources of truth. Would you say the Bible has been the source that leads you in all your ways? Describe how you recognize God's truth in your life.

_____

_____

_____

_____

_____

_____

_____

God, don't allow me to be led astray, but show me
Your truth and guide me by it. Amen.

GOD OF MY HOPE

Hope deferred makes the heart sick, but a longing fulfilled is a tree of life.

—PROVERBS 13:12 NIV

If you've been feeling like giving up, and if discouragement has clouded your vision, God wants to elevate your hope. He can do that if you put your hope in Him. He is never shaken, no matter what, and He is always faithful to His every promise. Cling to your hope in Him, and in His time, you will see your desires come to pass. Lift your eyes up; He never fails.

Take a moment to reflect: What or who have you clung to in hope? Has it caused you disappointment? What desires in your heart can you hand over to God today?

_____

_____

_____

_____

_____

_____

_____

God, You are my hope and my rock. You are who I cling to, and I know You will never disappoint me. Amen.

GOD'S WAY IS BETTER

When God fulfills your longings, sweetness fills your soul. But the wicked refuse to turn from darkness to see their desires come to pass.

—PROVERBS 13:19 TPT

Taking the "easy way out" always seems more enticing and inviting than waiting on God. That's when we start to impose our will instead of allowing God's will to run its course. As tempting as it may be to lead by our own compass, we must remember that God's way is better. God's timing is better. When we move in step with God, we'll be able to receive our dream with joy when it finally comes true.

_____

_____

_____

_____

_____

_____

_____

God, as badly as I may want this dream, I desire Your will for me more. I will wait for You and move in step with You. Amen.

LEAD ME

Direct me, Yahweh, throughout my journey so I can experience your plans for my life. Reveal the life-paths that are pleasing to you. Escort me into your truth; take me by the hand and teach me. For you are the God of my salvation.

—PSALM 25:4–5 TPT

Direct me. Lead me. Show me. This should be the heart's cry every single day, to involve and acknowledge God in all of our ways. From the smallest to the biggest areas of our lives, we should invite God into them, and His goodness and favor will surround us. Do you allow God to lead you, or have you preferred that He tag along? Take some time to invite God into your day.

_____

_____

_____

_____

_____

_____

_____

God, I surrender. I ask that You lead and guide me.
My life is Yours, so lead the way. Amen.

FOREVER PLAN

With his breath he scatters the schemes of nations who oppose him; they will never succeed. His destiny-plan for the earth stands sure. His forever-plan remains in place and will never fail.

—PSALM 33:10–11 TPT

God's plans always prevail. No matter who or what may rise against you, know that absolutely nothing can shake Him or His plans for you. Remember: "If God is for us, who can be against us?" (Romans 8:31 NIV). Replace your fear with confidence in the Lord. What has been shaking your faith lately? How does this verse encourage you to keep pressing forward?

_____

_____

_____

_____

_____

_____

God, no matter what may come, I believe that Your ways always prevail. I trust in You. Amen.

HE LIFTS YOU UP

When I said, "My foot is slipping," your unfailing love, Lord, supported me. When anxiety was great within me, your consolation brought me joy.

—PSALM 94:18–19 NIV

On your most difficult and trying days, God will sustain you. It may seem like all hope is lost and that you have failed, but God always has the final word, and He himself will lead you to triumph. He will hold you up when the world is weighing you down. God cares about what has been worrying you. Share that with Him today, and take some time to surrender all your anxieties to Him.

_____

_____

_____

_____

_____

_____

_____

God, even though I feel surrounded, I will look to You. Give me the strength I need to keep moving forward. Amen.

BURNOUT IS REAL

Even youths grow tired and weary, and young men stumble and fall; but those who hope in the Lord will renew their strength. They will soar on wings like eagles; they will run and not grow weary, they will walk and not be faint.

—ISAIAH 40:30–31 NIV

Burnout is real and God is aware of this. He knows that life can tire and drain you. Some constantly live in danger of burning out, and others avoid it because they have learned to pause and receive fresh strength from God. You have permission to rest in His presence, where you will find what you need. Are you often exhausted and always on the go? What can you change in your day that'll give you breaks and an opportunity to spend time with God?

_____

_____

_____

_____

_____

_____

God, give me rest in Your presence. Teach me to slow down and to receive my strength from You. Amen.

BOAST IN YAHWEH

Some find their strength in their weapons and wisdom, but my miracle-deliverance can never be won by men. Our boast is in Yahweh our God, who makes us strong and gives us victory!

—PSALM 20:7 TPT

Never count out the person who counts on God! While many may look to themselves and to their own resources, they will come to find that they are limited in power. The God of miracles, on the other hand, is unlimited in all His ways! May you boast of the Lord and not of yourself. Trust in Him and you'll see the mighty hand of God do wonderous works in your life. Have you ever relied more on your capabilities than God's? Did you struggle? Write about what you learned through that experience.

_____

_____

_____

_____

_____

_____

God, You are my reason to boast, and You are who makes me strong. It is You I lean on. Amen.

PRAISE THROUGH PROBLEMS

No matter what, I'll trust in you to help me. Nothing will stop me from praising you to magnify your glory!

—PSALM 71:14 TPT

This psalmist exemplifies someone who has put their complete trust in God. Even amidst problems, may you praise God even higher. Let it continue. You have a living hope within you. Make this your motto: "No matter what, I'll trust You." Is it difficult for you to praise God in the hard times? As you pray today, spend more time thanking God than thinking about problems, and watch everything shift.

God, no matter what may be happening in my life,
I will praise You, for You are always good. Amen.

EMBRACE FORGIVENESS

For all have sinned and fall short of the glory of God, and all are justified freely by his grace through the redemption that came by Christ Jesus.

ROMANS 3:23–24 NIV

In order to fully accept Jesus as our Savior, we have to recognize what we have been saved from. Jesus saved us from our sins. These sins had us chained in darkness, and they brought death and a guilty verdict upon us. But Jesus stepped in and brought us into the light, gave us life and freedom. You have permission to let go of the guilt and shame that sins produce and embrace the forgiveness and grace of Jesus. What has Jesus freed you from? Write about it.

_____

_____

_____

_____

_____

_____

Despite all my imperfections and sin, thank You, Jesus, for loving me anyway. Thank You for saving me and forgiving me. Amen.

COMPLETED WORK

Being confident of this, that he who began a good work in you will carry it on to completion until the day of Christ Jesus.

—PHILIPPIANS 1:6 NIV

God didn't bring you this far just to leave you behind. You can trust that whatever God begins, He completes. God never leaves anything unfinished, and God is not finished with you. He is doing something good in you, and right now He has you in the process of completion. The process may hurt, and you may not always understand His ways, but trust Him anyway. Do you ever grow frustrated with yourself in the process? Have you valued the result more than the walk to get there?

_____

_____

_____

_____

_____

_____

Father, finish whatever work You have begun in me and take me through whatever process as long as You are with me. Amen.

ONE ON ONE

Yes, my soul, find rest in God; my hope comes from him. Truly he is my rock and my salvation; he is my fortress, I will not be shaken.

—PSALM 62:5–6 NIV

There are real moments where everything in you wants to give in and give up. In this psalm, David pleads with his soul to breathe hope back in and to wait on God. He knows that hope is never wasted when it is placed on God. God alone is his rock, salvation, and fortress. God wants you to know Him in this way also so you can look to Him with expectant faith, knowing that everything is going to be okay. Have a real one-on-one with yourself just like David: What do you have to say to your soul today?

_____

_____

_____

_____

_____

_____

God, I desire to know You in this way. Would You come and be my rock, fortress, and salvation? I need You, Lord. Amen.

CREATOR OF HEARTS

The Lord looks over us from where he rules in heaven. Gazing into every heart from his lofty dwelling place, he observes all the peoples of the earth. The Creator of our hearts considers and examines everything we do.

—PSALM 33:13–15 TPT

If you ever find yourself questioning the plans God has for your life, remember this: The one who created your heart knows how to watch over your heart's desires. He is intimately aware of everything about you and all you do. Simply put, He who created you and watches over you knows what is best for you. Do you feel that you can trust God with your heart and your desires?

_____

_____

_____

_____

_____

_____

_____

_____

God, I trust You with my heart. Examine me and lead me. Amen.

UNTOLD BLESSINGS

If your faith remains strong, even while surrounded by life's difficulties, you will continue to experience the untold blessings of God!

—JAMES 1:12 TPT

We all face trials. Why not let God strengthen you through every struggle you find yourself up against? If you'll cling to God in the bad times, not letting your faith be shaken, He promises to bless you in wonderful ways. Take comfort in knowing that nothing hinders God's ability and desire to work for your good. How have you been blessed by keeping your faith in the darkness?

_____

_____

_____

_____

_____

_____

_____

God, help me cling to my faith in You today,
no matter what I face. Amen.

BLESS IT FORWARD

Those who live to bless others will have blessings heaped upon them, and the one who pours out his life to pour out blessings will be saturated with favor.

You can't go wrong with living to bless others. In fact, God will bless those who give generously. He is in the business of blessing His children. "Give generously and generous gifts will be given back to you, shaken down to make room for more . . . The measurement of your generosity becomes the measurement of your return" (Luke 6:38 TPT). Open up your hand to others and God will open His hand to you. What can you do today to bless and serve others?

_____

_____

_____

_____

_____

_____

God, make me a blessing to others. Teach me to live generously, always counting others as more significant than myself. Amen.

MAKE IT COUNT

Teach us to number our days, that we may gain a heart of wisdom.

PSALM 90:12 NIV

Paul tells us in Ephesians 5:15–16 (ESV) to "look carefully then how you walk, not as unwise but as wise, making the best use of the time." Every day that God gives is a gift and should be treated as such, never wasted. Pray, just as Moses did in Psalm 90:12, that God would grant you a heart of wisdom to best steward your day. Have you been mindful with your every day? How can you make the best use of your time today?

_____

_____

_____

_____

_____

_____

_____

God, give me wisdom to know how to go about my every day. Teach me how to steward my life well and to live it how You desire. Amen.

WORK AND HEAL

"Blessed is the one whom God corrects; so do not despise the discipline of the Almighty. For he wounds, but he also binds up; he injures, but his hands also heal."

—JOB 5:17–18 NIV

God's correction should be met not with pride but with a humble spirit. Don't run away from His counsel, because this is how He will make you walk in blessing. God corrects because He loves, and He desires to see His children grow and mature. Yearn for moments of discipline. Pray that God will expose areas in your heart that need healing. Has it ever been difficult to take God's correction? Are there areas God has pointed out that need work?

_____

_____

_____

_____

_____

_____

_____

_____

_____

God, You are my Father who loves me. Correct and discipline me. I desire to be more like You. Amen.

STEP CLOSER

I rise before dawn and cry for help; I have put my hope in your word.

Whoever seeks God with their whole heart will find Him. This psalmist desired to find God so he would "rise" to seek, "cry" in prayer, and "hope" in the Word. His actions echoed the yearning of his heart. You have access to God, and you can get as close as you would like. Do you desire a deeper relationship with God? What actions can you take to do that?

---

*God, I don't want a distant relationship with You.
Take me deeper into Your presence; I want
to know Your heart. Amen.*

HEAVENLY INHERITANCE

Don't allow the actions of evil men to cause you to burn with anger. Instead, burn with unrelenting passion as you worship God in holy awe.

—PROVERBS 23:17 TPT

Think about the wonderful gifts God has lavished you with. His Son, Jesus, made a way for salvation and eternal life. You have "an inheritance that is imperishable, undefiled, and unfading, kept in heaven for you" (1 Peter 1:4 ESV). Praise God for these gifts! Allow your heart to be filled with worship and refuse to let any bitterness or envy take root. Have you dealt with envy before, and how?

_____

_____

_____

_____

_____

_____

_____

God, remove any envy within me, and teach me to look to You and not to man. Amen.

DO GOOD

Let us not become weary in doing good, for at the proper time we will reap a harvest if we do not give up.

—GALATIANS 6:9 NIV

If you've ever thought "Maybe it's just not worth it," know today that Jesus is worth it. Don't give up just because there seems to be an easier way out or a shortcut. Sin is costly. But what God has to offer goes beyond anything you could ever imagine. Everything you are doing will reap a reward, so keep casting good seeds and prepare for the coming harvest. Do you ever get discouraged or tired of "doing good"?

_____

_____

_____

_____

_____

_____

_____

_____

_____

_____

God, give me endurance to keep moving forward.
Keep my eyes focused on You. Amen.

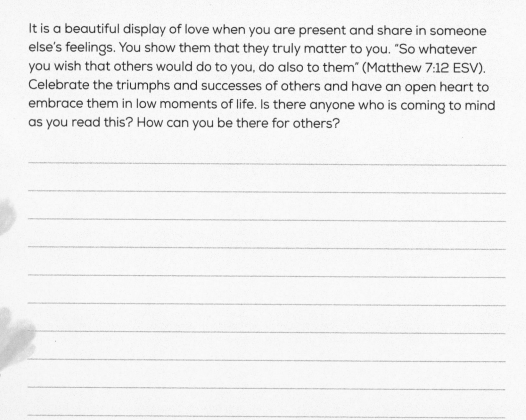

LOVE ON DISPLAY

Rejoice with those who rejoice; mourn with those who mourn.

—ROMANS 12:15 NIV

It is a beautiful display of love when you are present and share in someone else's feelings. You show them that they truly matter to you. "So whatever you wish that others would do to you, do also to them" (Matthew 7:12 ESV). Celebrate the triumphs and successes of others and have an open heart to embrace them in low moments of life. Is there anyone who is coming to mind as you read this? How can you be there for others?

_____

_____

_____

_____

_____

_____

_____

_____

_____

_____

_____

*God, bring blessing, favor, and opportunity
to my friends' lives. Amen.*

INTENTIONAL RELATIONSHIPS

Carry each other's burdens, and in this way you will fulfill the law of Christ.

—GALATIANS 6:2 NIV

Community is vital for the believer. My best friend once told me, "You win, I win. You lose, I lose." That day she brought this verse from Galatians to life, and I learned that friendships need to be treated with intentionality and care. We are called to love, encourage, and lift one another up. Remember that to have a good friend, you have to be a good friend. What values do you look for in a friend? Do you reflect these values in your own life?

_____

_____

_____

_____

_____

_____

_____

_____

_____

God, help me have godly relationships, and make me a better friend to serve and love like You do. Amen.

MAKE EACH OTHER BETTER

As iron sharpens iron, so one person sharpens another.

—PROVERBS 27:17 NIV

Iron cannot sharpen itself; another piece of iron is necessary for both to be effective and ready for their intended use. We can apply this illustration to our relationships, too. Just think about who you have around you. Walk with those who will offer godly advice, encourage you, pray with you, and, above all, love you. Consider your relationships: Are you making one another better? Pray for relationships that will serve to grow and sharpen you.

_____

_____

_____

_____

_____

_____

_____

_____

_____

_____

_____

*God, teach me to be a good friend who
loves and serves well. Amen.*

COME ANYWAY

Lord, you know all my desires and deepest longings. My tears are liquid words, and you can read them all . . . Lord, the only thing I can do is wait and put my hope in you. I wait for your help, my God.

—PSALM 38:9, 15 TPT

If all you have are tears, that's okay; come to God anyway. If showing up is all you can do, that's okay. That's all He needs. Be still in His presence and wait for His help. He is with you through it all, and He will turn your sorrow into joy. Do difficult seasons often discourage you from seeking God? How might you overcome?

_____

_____

_____

_____

_____

_____

God, no matter what the circumstance or what my feelings are, I will come to You because You are my peace and my hope. Amen.

HOPE AND ENDURE

Whatever was written beforehand is meant to instruct us in how to live. The Scriptures impart to us encouragement and inspiration so that we can live in hope and endure all things.

—ROMANS 15:4 TPT

The Bible does not showcase a bunch of perfect people who had it all figured out; it shares the story of a mighty God amidst imperfect people who love Him. All of them are very different, have their own weaknesses, and experience many ups and downs. Through their testimonies we can learn to hope and endure. The same God who delivered them is with you now.. The Bible can serve you hope and encouragement through their stories. Is there anyone from the Bible that you identify with? What do they teach you?

_____

_____

_____

_____

_____

_____

God, reveal Your Word to me and teach me how to endure.
May I receive encouragement through You. Amen.

FULFILL YOUR PURPOSE

You keep every promise you've ever made to me! Since your love for me is constant and endless, I ask you, Lord, to finish every good thing that you've begun in me!

—PSALM 138:8 TPT

Be encouraged that no matter what has happened, God has not changed His mind about you. God intends to fulfill the purpose He set for you. He keeps His promises, and His plans stand forever! Have you ever thought your mistakes derailed God's plan for you? How might you overcome these beliefs?

_____

_____

_____

_____

_____

_____

_____

_____

_____

God, Your plans are perfect and beautiful.
Your promises sustain me. Amen.

HE IS GRACIOUS

Yet the Lord longs to be gracious to you; therefore he will rise up to show you compassion. For the Lord is a God of justice. Blessed are all who wait for him!

—ISAIAH 30:18 NIV

"God, why is it taking so long? When will You finally do what You promised?" Do you ever find yourself asking such questions of God? While we are so caught up in the why and when, God is concerned with the what and how. There is a purpose behind the wait, and the process of getting there is refining you. The wait is God extending grace to you. Do you struggle to trust God's timing?

_____

_____

_____

_____

_____

_____

_____

God, I know You have perfect timing; help me with my impatience and remove my doubts so that I may trust You and Your timing. Amen.

OBEDIENCE AND BLESSING

When he had finished speaking, he said to Simon, "Put out into deep water, and let down the nets for a catch."

—LUKE 5:4 NIV

After an unsuccessful and grueling night of fishing, Jesus requests that Simon go deeper into the water and cast his nets. When he cast his nets, there was abundance to the point that the nets were breaking, and the boats began to sink because of all the fish. Alone, Simon was unsuccessful. With Jesus, he experienced blessing. Can you identify areas in your life where you need to go deeper? How can you be more obedient to the Lord?

_____

_____

_____

_____

_____

_____

_____

_____

_____

_____

Jesus, teach me to trust and obey You even when I don't understand. Allow me to see You work miracles in and through my life. Amen.

EVERLASTING LOVE

"I have loved you with an everlasting love; I have drawn you with unfailing kindness."

—JEREMIAH 31:3 NIV

You can be assured of God's constant and never-ending love for you. It can't be earned or lost, because love is who God is. Even when His children show themselves to be unfaithful, He remains who He is and is always faithful. He waits with open arms to receive His children. Have you ever felt that you needed to earn God's love? How did that make you view Him?

_____

_____

_____

_____

_____

_____

_____

_____

_____

God, I praise You for Your unfailing love. Thank You
for never walking out on me. Amen.

ALL AT ONCE

Fully awake, he rebuked the storm and shouted to the sea, "Hush! Be still!" All at once the wind stopped howling and the water became perfectly calm.

—MARK 4:39 TPT

One word from Jesus can shift everything around you. When thoughts are running rampant, His words bring peace. When doubts are clouding your vision, His Word brings clarity. Instead of running to fear, run to His Word. Take this space to ask God to speak to you, and ask Him to open your heart to hear from Him.

_____

_____

_____

_____

_____

_____

_____

God, give me a receiving heart so that I may know You through Your Word. Amen.

LOOK TO JESUS

Let us throw off everything that hinders and the sin that so easily entangles. And let us run with perseverance the race marked out for us.

—HEBREWS 12:1 NIV

Running this race requires the right perspective. As you go about your daily life, no matter what may come, keep your eyes focused on Jesus. Distractions will come and situations will arise that will aim to take you off course, but as you look to Jesus, He will supply and perfect your faith. It's important to recognize what hinders us, and sins often get in the way of our race. What might those be for you?

_____

_____

_____

_____

_____

_____

_____

_____

God, help me keep my eyes fixed on You and remove anything that gets in the way of following you. Amen.

SAY THE RIGHT WORDS

Everyone enjoys giving great advice. But how delightful it is to say the right thing at the right time!

—PROVERBS 15:23 TPT

Have you ever wished for a do-over in instances where you spoke too quickly or unwisely? "Death and life are in the power of the tongue" (Proverbs 18:21 KJV). Your words possess this power when you give advice. If someone has trusted you for counsel, be thoughtful and prayerful about your words. Be someone people can count on for life-giving advice. Have you ever received life-changing advice?

_____

_____

_____

_____

_____

_____

_____

_____

*God, give me wisdom to speak, and may the advice
I give echo Your Word. Amen.*

FOLLOW THE LEADER

"My sheep listen to my voice; I know them, and they follow me."

—JOHN 10:27 NIV

Sheep follow the shepherd with no questions asked. They trust the shepherd's leadership because they know that he cares for, leads, and guides them. The goal of the believer should be the same: to be attentive to the voice of Jesus and to follow Him wherever He may lead. Does Jesus have your complete trust? Examine your life. Do you actually allow Jesus to lead and shepherd you?

_____

_____

_____

_____

_____

_____

_____

_____

_____

_____

_____

God, give me a responsive heart to Your voice.
You can lead and I will follow. Amen.

COMPLETELY CONNECTED

Jesus gave them this answer: "Very truly I tell you, the Son can do nothing by himself; he can do only what he sees his Father doing, because whatever the Father does the Son also does."

—JOHN 5:19 NIV

Jesus always leads by example and never asks us to do anything He hasn't done. In this verse, He shows His full submission to the Father's will and acknowledges His need for Him. Jesus shows this complete connection that He has with the Father. We are to live this way also and be dependent on God. Do you live your life this way? Explore your answer and the reasons why below.

_____

_____

_____

_____

_____

_____

_____

God, make me completely connected to You, and rid me of any self-sufficiency. I need You. Amen.

TAKE A BREAK

There was such a swirl of activity around Jesus, with so many people coming and going, that they were unable to even eat a meal. So Jesus said to his disciples, "Come, let's take a break and find a secluded place where you can rest a while."

—MARK 6:31 TPT

Days can get so busy; perhaps you understand what Jesus is talking about here. In the busyness and chaos going on, the disciples didn't even have time to eat. However, Jesus recognized they needed to break away from the chaos and get time alone to rest. In the same way, you need rest, even if it is for a few minutes. Get time alone with God and allow Him to replenish your strength and renew you. Think about your schedule. How can you prioritize time with God?

_____

_____

_____

_____

_____

God, in the busyness of my day, give me a yearning to be alone in Your presence. Amen.

ALWAYS WITH YOU

If I fly with wings into the shining dawn, you're there! If I fly into the radiant sunset, you're there waiting!

—PSALM 139:9 TPT

The safest place you can be in is the hands of God. No matter where life leads you to go or calls you to stay, you can trust that God will be with you every single moment. Meet future endeavors with faith and confidence that the Father will never leave you. What does knowing that God never leaves you do to your heart?

_____

_____

_____

_____

_____

_____

_____

_____

Father God, just knowing You are always with me showers me with peace. Thank You, God. Amen.

LIFE-CHANGING DECISION

Because I set you, Yahweh, always close to me, my confidence will never be weakened, for I experience your wraparound presence every moment.

—PSALM 16:8 TPT

David made a decision in this verse: God was going to be the focus of his heart. He knew he needed to make God first in his life. Making God your everything changes everything! He begins to work in you, on your attitude and your outlook on life. Have you put God first in your life, or does He often become an afterthought?

_____

_____

_____

_____

_____

_____

_____

Lord God, I have decided to set my heart and mind on You.
All I desire is to be close to You. Amen.

SLEEP IN THE STORM

So now I'll lie down and sleep like a baby—then I'll awake in safety, for you surround me with your glory.

—PSALM 3:5 TPT

David wrote this psalm amidst distress and betrayal from those close to him. He'd even been wronged by his very own blood, his son Absalom. His faith in God let him embrace peace in the storm. Just as God's love is unconditional, so is the peace He gives to His children. Have you lost sleep because worry, anxiety, or fear got the better of you? God wants to welcome you into rest today and bring peace into your heart, mind, and body.

_____

_____

_____

_____

_____

_____

_____

_____

_____

Father God, I surrender any worry that has been overtaking my mind lately. Bring Your peace over my life. Amen.

UNWELCOME GUEST

Put me to the test and sift through all my anxious cares.

—PSALM 139:23 TPT

David invited the Lord to step into the depths of His heart to uncover all that had him under the rule of anxiousness. It was no longer welcome, so he asked God to expose it and bring it to the light. Whatever situations may have you downcast and filled with worry, God wants to help you deal with them. Is there anything in your life that has been weighing you down?

_____

_____

_____

_____

_____

_____

_____

_____

_____

Father God, do the work that only You can do in my heart. Expose anything that does not belong and bring Your rule over it. Amen.

GOD IS NOT FINISHED

My flesh and my heart may fail, but God is the strength of my heart and my portion forever.

—*PSALM 73:26 NIV*

God has given us a reason to get up, try again, and keep going. He is the reason and the hope of our heart! People may fail—you may even fail yourself—but God never will. If you're feeling weary, allow God to fill you with strength. God is not finished with you. Have you ever felt discouraged to continue following God because of repeated mistakes?

_____

_____

_____

_____

_____

_____

_____

_____

Father God, You are my strength in the midst of weakness.
You alone give me hope to keep pushing forward.
Your presence is all I need. Amen.

WORDS STICK

Reckless words are like the thrusts of a sword, cutting remarks meant to stab and to hurt. But the words of the wise soothe and heal.

—PROVERBS 12:18 TPT

Has someone ever said hurtful or hateful things to you? Those kinds of words leave a sting and at times stay as a permanent memory in your mind. The words you say to others also hold the same power. Your words can be either a sword for piercing and scarring or a medicine for healing. Do you struggle with speaking too quickly and out of emotion at times?

_____

_____

_____

_____

_____

_____

_____

_____

Father God, give me wisdom when I speak and teach me what to say. Help me love others well. Amen.

LET GO OF FEAR

But in the day that I'm afraid, I lay all my fears before you and trust in you with all my heart.

—PSALM 56:3 TPT

The same David who defeated the giant Goliath wrote this psalm about fear. It's not that David was fearless; it's that his trust in God was greater than anything he faced. He discovered the same secret as Paul: "I can do all things through him who strengthens me" (Philippians 4:13 ESV). Confession brings liberation. What fears do you struggle with?

_____

_____

_____

_____

_____

_____

_____

Father God, I lay before You all my fears, and I trust that You are greater than them all. I will no longer allow them to overtake me. If You are with me, what can be against me? Amen.

LOVING FATHER

Yet still, Yahweh, you are our Father. We are like clay and you are our Potter. Each one of us is the creative, artistic work of your hands.

—ISAIAH 64:8 TPT

A loving father never forgets his children. God is a good father to His children, and He desires to see them grow and become all He intended for them. He desires for you to know His heart of a father. You'll see that giving yourself completely to this love is the greatest decision you could ever make, and you will be the work of His loving hand. How has God shown Himself to be a father to you?

_____

_____

_____

_____

_____

_____

_____

_____

*God, reveal to me more of Your heart, and show me
who You are as my Father. Amen.*

LIVE SECURE

They will not live in fear or dread of what may come, for their hearts are firm, ever secure in their faith.

—PSALM 112:7 TPT

We live in a world full of unknowns, and that can keep many locked in a cage of fear. This fear can keep you unmotivated and unwilling to face the day ahead. Don't miss out on the gift of life that God has granted you. He desires for you to have abundant life and walk with the confidence that you are fully secure in His hands. Fear does not have a hold on you, so take back the life that God purposed for you. What opportunities has God placed before you? How will you place them in His hands?

_____

_____

_____

_____

_____

_____

_____

God, every day I ask that You hold my hand through life.
I rebuke any fear that keeps me from living in the purpose
You have for me. In Jesus' name, amen.

YOU ARE NOT ALONE

Because you are my help, I sing in the shadow of your wings.

—PSALM 63:7 NIV

Have you ever felt that your worship has been hindered because you are going through trials and difficulties? The moments that drive you away are the moments you are to cling to God all the more. Allow Him to be your reason to sing, to feel joy, and to hope again. You are not alone; God will be your "refuge and strength, always ready to help in times of trouble" (Psalm 46:1 NLT). There's no shadow of a doubt under the shadow of His wings. What are the areas of your life where you need to invite God to be your help?

_____

_____

_____

_____

_____

_____

_____

God, You have always been there for me. I know You will
complete everything You have started in me.
Even when I feel like I can't, I know that You can.
You are my help. Amen.

MADE FOR THE MOMENT

"And who knows but that you have come to your royal position for such a time as this?"

—ESTHER 4:14 NIV

God took an orphaned outcast and positioned her as a queen fit to execute His divine plan. Through her life, God thwarted the enemy's plan to do away with His chosen people. Esther was made for that moment, and she responded in obedience. You, much like Esther, were made by God for such a time as this. Step into your moment, confident in the purposes of God. Does the feeling of inadequacy often keep you from stepping out in faith?

_____

_____

_____

_____

_____

_____

_____

God, I have often feared that I am not good enough and not qualified for the task in front of me. Remove those thoughts from me and complete Your purpose for my life. Amen.

NO MISTAKES

And he marked out their appointed times in history and the boundaries of their lands. God did this so that they would seek him and perhaps reach out for him and find him, though he is not far from any one of us.

—ACTS 17:26–27 NIV

If you've ever thought you were an accident, God desires for you to know that you are an intentional creation. Before you were formed in your mother's womb, He knew you (Jeremiah 1:5). Your where and when were determined by God as His divine plan anchored at the mission that you would seek and know Him. The big and small details all together tell the story of God in your life. What evidence of God have you seen in your life?

_____

_____

_____

_____

_____

_____

_____

God, give me eyes to see Your fingerprint all over my life. Remind me that I am Your creation, made with and for a purpose. Pull me closer to You. Amen.

IF ONLY

Martha said to Jesus, "My Lord, if only you had come sooner, my brother wouldn't have died."

—JOHN 11:21 TPT

Have you ever felt like God let you down? Martha knew this feeling, too. Her brother had died, and Jesus showed up four days too late. But Jesus went on to perform a miracle, and her brother Lazarus was resurrected. Where there had been no hope there was now life, testimony, faith, and glory for God. Can you relate to Martha and what she was feeling?

_____

_____

_____

_____

_____

_____

_____

_____

God, hold my heart steady, keep my mind fixed on You, and help me avoid leaning on my own understanding of what is possible. You are the God of miracles! Amen.

DIVINE APPOINTMENT

That night the king could not sleep; so he ordered the book of the chronicles, the record of his reign, to be brought in and read to him.

—ESTHER 6:1 NIV

During a night of tossing and turning, King Xerxes decided to have a book of records read to him. Little did he know that God was about to use that moment to accomplish His purposes. That moment would eventually lead to the salvation of God's people. God uses different methods and moments to speak to us. An ordinary moment, a sleepless night, can be turned into a divine appointment. If God is prompting your spirit, don't ignore it. He is desiring to accomplish His purposes. What do you do with your sleepless nights?

_____

_____

_____

_____

_____

_____

God, prompt my spirit to be able to discern when You want to meet with me. I desire to hear from You and see Your hand work in my life. Amen.

DIVINE MYSTERIES

As you do not know the path of wind, or how the body is formed in a mother's womb, so you cannot understand the work of God, the Maker of all things.

—ECCLESIASTES 11:5 NIV

The hidden things of life tell the story of the grandeur of God. He is mighty in power, infinite in knowledge, and wonderful in all His ways. We have not been called to decipher the ways of God, or to have all the answers; our part is to trust Him. How do you respond to the unknown in your life?

_____

_____

_____

_____

_____

_____

_____

_____

God, help me remember that You are in control. You hold the world and my life in Your hand. Amen.

YOU CAN DO ALL THINGS

"I know that you can do all things; no purpose of yours can be thwarted."

—JOB 42:2 NIV

Job makes a confession to God in the midst of loss, doubt, and turmoil within his heart. He realizes nothing can stop the purposes of God. The plans of God are sure, even when the season is unpredictable and confusing. Are there situations you are facing that you have made to seem greater than God?

_____

_____

_____

_____

_____

_____

_____

_____

Father God, You are greater than my current situation.
Nothing placed before me will stop Your purposes.
I know You can do all things. Amen.

ENLIGHTEN MY WAYS

Listen to my counsel, for my instruction will enlighten you.
You'll be wise not to ignore it.

Yearn for the wisdom of God. Open your heart to be instructed, molded, and directed by Him. Blessing, favor, and direction can all be found through His counsel. Make wisdom the center of your thoughts and prayers today. What area in your life do you desire God's counsel in?

_____

_____

_____

_____

_____

_____

_____

_____

_____

God, I turn to You today and ask for wisdom. Speak to
me so I may learn and grow. Amen.

OPEN THE WORD

Break open your Word within me until revelation-light shines out! Those with open hearts are given insight into your plans.

—PSALM 119:130 TPT

Just as the light shines your way, so does the Word of God. The Bible is living and active! If you ask the Lord for revelation, He delights in giving it. He searches for those with open hearts that are receptive to His counsel. If you've been asking God for guidance over a decision, or maybe need clarity about what your next step should be, His Word has the answer. Is there an area in your life that needs clarity? Write about it below, asking God for wisdom.

_____

_____

_____

_____

_____

_____

_____

_____

God, show me the way by revealing Your Word to me.
May it bring the clarity and guidance I need. Amen.

COME BOLDLY

Let us approach God's throne of grace with confidence, so that we may receive mercy and find grace to help us in our time of need.

—HEBREWS 4:16 NIV

Have you ever viewed God as unapproachable? Or maybe shame has taken root, and you've thought that God doesn't want to hear from you. Jesus made a way for us; we can now come before the throne confidently. The Father desires to hear from you! No matter where you've been or what you've done, come boldly. He is always available and ready to help in times of need.

_____

_____

_____

_____

_____

_____

_____

Father God, thank You for hearing me when I draw near.
You are always there for me as my loving Father. Amen.

DON'T GIVE UP

Here's what I've learned through it all: Don't give up;
don't be impatient; be entwined as one with the Lord. Be
brave and courageous, and never lose hope. Yes, keep on
waiting—for he will never disappoint you!

PSALM 27:14 TPT

In the midst of trials it is easy to feel alone, and it is difficult to find courage within yourself to keep on going. When you live completely connected to God, the story is much different. You then look to Him for the hope you cannot find in trying circumstances. You find the will to keep moving forward because you know that God has already gone before you. You find peace because He has taught you to endure and to be patient. Think about your life for a moment; have you been looking within yourself or to other things to give you what only God can bring?

_____

_____

_____

_____

_____

God, teach me to endure life's circumstances as I look to
You for strength. Keep me away from self-dependency.
In You I find all that I need. Amen.

DELIVERING GOD

In my distress I cried out to you, the delivering God, and from your temple-throne you heard my troubled cry, and my sobs went right into your heart.

—PSALM 18:6 TPT

When you're feeling at your weakest and lowest, that is not the time to run away from God but to run to Him. God is not looking for you to present your best self to Him; He wants the real you. He welcomes those who are tired, weary, broken, distressed—you name it. He is able to deliver and rescue you from it all. Have you avoided God before because you felt you weren't good enough to face Him?

Lord, at times I hide my face from You, feeling as if I cannot come into Your presence because everything surrounding me is just too messy. Remind me that You aren't scared of my mess; rather, You are there waiting to help pick up the pieces. Amen.

FULL OF POWER

"Not one promise from God is empty of power. Nothing is impossible with God!"

—LUKE 1:37 TPT

This is a reminder for your soul today from the heart of the Father: Nothing is impossible with God! Maybe what is before you right now *seems* impossible. Maybe you see no way out and no capacity within yourself to get it done. The good news is that God will not leave you to deal with it on your own. God is on it, and He is with you. His promises are full of power, so if God said it, believe it! Do you have trouble believing in the promises of God in the midst of difficulty?

_____

_____

_____

_____

_____

_____

God, I believe in Your promises. I believe in You more than what my eyes see. You are greater than any circumstance or experience that I have to go through. Nothing is impossible with You by my side. Amen.

TRUST AND BELIEVE

"Do not let your hearts be troubled. You believe in God; believe also in me."

—JOHN 14:1 NIV

God has not called you to live in fear or worry but to live in freedom and hope. Don't allow your current circumstance to shake your faith or rob your peace. Friend, God is greater than any problem before you. Believe and trust in God; He is making a way even if you don't see it. Can you trust God to handle your current situations?

_____

_____

_____

_____

_____

_____

_____

*God, I surrender my life's issues to You in this moment.
I know that You are with me and You will take
care of it. I trust and believe in You. Amen.*

MIRACLE-DELIVERANCE

When I had nothing, desperate and defeated, I cried out to the Lord and he heard me, bringing his miracle-deliverance when I needed it most.

—PSALM 34:6 TPT

In moments where your spirit is feeling defeated and desperate, not knowing who or what to turn to, run into the Father's arms. Seek Him, cry out to Him, because He hears you and He will deliver you! What do you need most right now? Let God know and step into a moment with Him.

_____

_____

_____

_____

_____

_____

_____

God, in my moments of defeat, remind me that victory is in You.
I will turn to You in my times of need. Listen to
my cries and deliver me from my despair. Amen.

GUILT GO AWAY

Whenever our hearts make us feel guilty and remind us of our failures, *we know that God is much greater* and more merciful *than our conscience, and he knows everything there is to know* about us.

—1 JOHN 3:20 TPT

For every time that guilt comes upon you or shame wants to creep in and make you feel unworthy, remind yourself of this truth: God loves you! His love is greater than any feeling. You are an open book before Him; there is nothing in your past, present, or even your future that is enough to wear out His love for you! Even if your heart tells you that you're guilty, God has called you innocent. Do you struggle with shame? Has it kept you from deepening your relationship with God?

_____

_____

_____

_____

Father, I know that shame does not come from You, so teach me to live in Your forgiveness. May Your truth be the anchor of my life. Amen.

GOODNESS AND LOVE

So why would I fear the future? *Only goodness and tender love pursue me all the days of my life.*

—PSALM 23:6 TPT

Your future is secure in the hands of God. Because of Him you can meet every single day with faith. Don't allow fear of the future to rob you of seeing the goodness and love that God has set apart for you today. Give Him your today and your tomorrow. What scares you about the future?

_____

_____

_____

_____

_____

_____

_____

_____

Father God, I know that You are in control of it all. My tomorrows belong to You, so help me live in the moment so I may experience Your overwhelming goodness. Amen.

ONE THING

*Here's the one thing I crave from Yahweh, the one thing
I seek above all else: I want to live with him every moment
in his house, beholding the marvelous beauty of Yahweh,
filled with awe, delighting in his glory and grace. I want to
contemplate in his temple.*

—PSALM 27:4 TPT

The posture of the believer's heart is found in this verse. People constantly seek fulfillment, meaning, and happiness, trying one thing after the other to try to find them. One taste of the presence of God could bring all of this. David understood the value of God, and it isn't reserved just for him but also available to you and me. Endless joy and privileges are found in Him. What occupies the first place in your heart?

_____

_____

_____

_____

_____

*God, consume my heart with Your love; may You be
the center of it. Show me who You are. Amen.*

GOD IS FOR YOU

Out of my deep anguish and pain I prayed, and God, you helped me as a father. You came to my rescue and broke open the way into a beautiful and broad place. Now I know, Lord, that you are for me, and I will never fear what man can do to me.

—PSALM 118:5–6 TPT

Moments of pain and experiences of distress teach us that even in our worst moments, God doesn't walk away. He moves even closer. The struggles prove that God is for us, because somehow, He always makes a way. When you face a difficulty, remember: If God pulled you out of that mess, then He will do it again now. God will never fail you. Think about a hard moment you went through; what did God teach you through it?

_____

_____

_____

_____

_____

*Thank You, God, because with You victory is sure.
Struggles may come and difficulties will rise, but my eyes
will be set on You. You always make a way. Amen.*

WELL DONE

"His master replied, 'Well done, good and faithful servant! You have been faithful with a few things; I will put you in charge of many things. Come and share your master's happiness!'"

—MATTHEW 25:23 NIV

Make this the motivation for your life, that one day you will hear these beautiful words from the Savior. With a pleased expression He will say, "Well done." No matter what may happen today, keep this as the focus of your heart and mind; these are the words you are living for. Keep walking with God and don't lose heart. Take time to commit your day to God and express to Him whatever is on your heart.

_____

_____

_____

_____

_____

_____

Father God, steady my heart to keep focused on You and the day I will see You face-to-face. Teach me to live with an eternal perspective. Amen.

WRAP MY HEART

Don't ever say, "I'm going to get even with them if it's the last thing I do!" Wrap God's grace around your heart and he will be the one to vindicate you.

—PROVERBS 20:22 TPT

God has heard how people have spoken of you, and He has seen how they have hurt you. God doesn't want hate or resentment to even enter your heart and keep you chained to the past; He wants to see you living free and full. You can choose grace over anger, because you live in the peace of knowing that God will take care of it all in His way. Remember, as much as you may want to even the score, God's vindication is better than your revenge. Are you struggling with forgiving others? Or with resentment? Release those feelings to God today and allow peace to fill your heart.

_____

_____

_____

_____

God, give me a heart that forgives the way that You do. Remove any traces of resentment or bitterness that have taken root in me. God, although they have hurt me, I release them to You today. I no longer want to live angry. I choose grace. Amen.

GOD'S PURPOSE ALWAYS SUCCEEDS

A person may have many ideas concerning God's plan for his life, but only the designs of God's purpose will succeed in the end.

—PROVERBS 19:21 TPT

At times, we can hold our dreams with tight fists, believing that we know the best steps to get to where we've always imagined ourselves to be. But the best step you can take is to hand over your dreams to God, who is the designer and builder of your life. You can trust that He will not disappoint. Only He knows how to truly fulfil the longings of your heart. Have you truly surrendered your plans to God?

_____

_____

_____

_____

_____

_____

_____

_____

Dear Lord, in all of my pursuits and plans, I pray that Your purpose for my life will be revealed. Amen.

FIXED PURPOSE

Set your gaze on the path before you. With fixed purpose, looking straight ahead, ignore life's distractions. Watch where you're going! Stick to the path of truth, and the road will be safe and smooth before you.

—PROVERBS 4:25–26 TPT

Friend, you are a child of God who has been made with and for a purpose. Although there may be many distractions trying to pull you away from your destiny, choose God daily. Commit your heart and way to Him and He will make your path straight. What distractions have been pulling at your attention lately?

_____

_____

_____

_____

_____

_____

_____

Father God, as many distractions come my way today, steady my heart to keep looking to You. Teach me to be watchful and cautious with all that is around me. Amen.

WORDS OF FAITH

Their wounding words pierce my heart over and over while they say, "Where is this God of yours?" So I say to my soul, "Don't be discouraged. Don't be disturbed. For I know my God will break through for me."

—PSALM 42:10–11 TPT

In the midst of discouragement, the voices and opinions of those around you seem to get louder. They may even begin to ridicule or mock your faith. It's in these moments where you must choose the truth of God's Word and drown out the lies. Speak words of faith into your soul and remind yourself of the mighty works of God to encourage your Spirit. What can you say to yourself to help face the day before you?

God, help me remember who You are in the midst of difficulty and rejection. May You be the only voice of truth that directs me. You are my confidence; it is You who I look to. Amen.

LIFE-GIVING WORD

Anxious fear brings depression, but a life-giving word of encouragement can do wonders to restore joy to the heart.

—PROVERBS 12:25 TPT

The words within you can breathe life back into a person and restore their joy. Pray that your words carry hope and bring light in the midst of darkness. God has called you to serve and love those around you; open yourself up to be used by God. As you're reading this, is there anyone that God is placing on your heart? Write their name and a prayer for them and be encouraged to reach out to them. There's a reason they are coming to mind.

_____

_____

_____

_____

_____

_____

_____

Father God, make me aware of the people around me. Help me love them better and share Your promises with them. Amen.

GOD IS MY STRENGTH

By your mighty power I can walk through any devastation, and you will keep me alive, reviving me. Your power set me free from the hatred of my enemies. You keep every promise you've ever made to me!

—PSALM 138:7-8 TPT

The person who makes God their confidence can stand fearless in the day of trouble, as they are not discouraged by the impossibility of a situation. When you feel powerless, look to God and He will revive you and supply you with strength. Don't allow situations to get the best of you, because you know that God has a hold of you. Do you look to God as your source of strength?

_____

_____

_____

_____

_____

_____

Lord, fill me with strength and confidence to face all that is before me. Give me faith to keep a hold of Your promises even in difficult moments. Amen.

DO NOT WORRY

Jesus taught his disciples, saying, "Listen to me. Never let anxiety enter your hearts. Never worry about any of your needs . . . Does worry add anything to your life? Can it add one more year, or even one day? So if worrying adds nothing, but actually subtracts from your life, why would you worry about God's care of you?"

—LUKE 12:22, 25 TPT

Truly ask yourself whether worry is adding anything to your life. I'd say it's actually stripping away your peace and health. Worry may bring doubt where there used to be faith. God wants you to live at rest, knowing that you are secure and taken care of by Him. You are His child and He is your loving Father; His eyes are ever on you and He will provide for your every need. What are your worries today? Leave them at His feet and allow His peace to come over you.

_____

_____

_____

_____

Father God, help me release any anxiety that has entered my heart. I surrender my worries to You today. I believe that You are my protector and sustainer. Amen.

FREEDOM IN CONFESSION

Then I finally admitted to you all my sins, refusing to hide them any longer. I said, "My life-giving God, I will openly acknowledge my evil actions." And you forgave me!
All at once the guilt of my sin washed away and all my pain disappeared!

—PSALM 32:5 TPT

Hidden sin is the breeding ground of shame and guilt. It's what keeps you in a cage, feeling unworthy of the love of God, and keeps your relationship with Him from flourishing. There is freedom available for you today. Come before God, acknowledge your shortcomings, and allow His forgiveness and love to wash over you. Are there any sins, from your past or present, that you have been struggling with?

_____

_____

_____

_____

_____

Father God, forgive me of all of my sins. Wash me clean and make me new. In Jesus' name, amen.

TESTIMONY OF GRACE

As for you, you were dead in your transgressions and sins, in which you used to live when you followed the ways of this world . . . But because of his great love for us, God, who is rich in mercy, made us alive with Christ even when we were dead in transgressions—it is by grace you have been saved.

—EPHESIANS 2:1–2, 4–5 NIV

Only God can turn a story of death into a testimony of grace! You are living proof of the love and mercy of God; He has made you completely new. Embrace the walk you have been on and testify to those around you about the work that God has done in you and the redemption that is available for them also. What is your story? What did He save you from?

_____

_____

_____

_____

_____

God, thank You for rewriting my story and saving me.
Your love has saved me from death and
has given me a new life! Amen.

MORE THAN READY

Yes, God is more than ready to overwhelm you with every form of grace, so that you will have more than enough of everything—every moment and in every way. He will make you overflow with abundance in every good thing you do.

—2 CORINTHIANS 9:8 TPT

For the days when worry begins to cloud over your faith, and you feel unsure about how you will make ends meet or if you have the right resources to make the dream happen, remember that God is your sustainer and way-maker. Faith doesn't mean you have it all figured out; it means that you can trust in God even when you don't know what comes next. If God has placed a dream within you, rest assured that He will supply you with all you need and will open the right doors to get you there. Are you trying to go through life by playing it safe, or are you walking by faith?

_____

_____

_____

_____

_____

God, help me look to You as my sustainer, and teach me to trust in Your promises more than I trust in my own resources. Amen.

PLANTED BY GOD'S DESIGN

He will be standing firm like a flourishing tree planted by God's design, deeply rooted by the brooks of bliss, bearing fruit in every season of life. He is never dry, never fainting, ever blessed, ever prosperous.

—PSALM 1:3 TPT

The one who follows God's ways is not easily swayed by trends, moved because of trials, or distracted because of temptation. They choose obedience not out of obligation but out of love, and they have found that living surrendered before God has brought them freedom. They are connected to the One who always supplies no matter what the season may be, and who gives them the strength to keep moving forward. Take a moment to think of your life and tendencies. Are you walking with God or living according to your desires?

_____

_____

_____

_____

_____

Father God, connect me to Your heart. May nothing that comes my way move me away. Teach me to lean on You and stay with You through it all. Amen.

CHOOSE GRACE

Watch over each other to make sure that no one misses the revelation of God's grace. And make sure no one lives with a root of bitterness sprouting within them which will only cause trouble and poison the hearts of many.

—HEBREWS 12:15 TPT

Have you noticed that at times it takes just a small inconvenience or a bad moment to derail your whole day? A 5-minute conversation can end up taking over your mood for the next 12 hours. We have an active choice every day to pick up grace or allow bitterness to take root within us. Bitterness is a poison that spreads, taking life from you and those around you. Choose the grace and goodness that God has available for you today. How do you usually respond to inconveniences that happen during your day?

_____

_____

_____

_____

_____

_____

Father, help me choose grace instead of bitterness so that I may focus on the joy that You have set before me. Amen.

WHO DO YOU SAY THAT I AM?

"But what about you?" he asked. "Who do you say I am?"
Simon Peter answered, "You are the Messiah, the Son of
the living God."

—MATTHEW 16:15–16 NIV

Jesus asked His disciples who people thought He was, and they had heard people thought Him to be John the Baptist, Elijah, or one of the prophets. Jesus then turned His focus to His disciples themselves. He wanted to know who they believed He was, and Peter gave this beautiful answer: that Jesus is the Son of God. Peter knew Jesus personally because he walked with Him. In the same way, Jesus desires for you to know Him personally and intimately, not just through what other people may say or believe. Who do you say Jesus is? Who do you know Him to be?

_____

_____

_____

_____

_____

Lord, reveal to me more of who You are. I desire to know
Your heart and have a deeper relationship with You. Amen.

GOD EQUIPS

Moses said to the Lord, "Pardon your servant, Lord. I have never been eloquent, neither in the past nor since you have spoken to your servant. I am slow of speech and tongue."

—EXODUS 4:10 NIV

As God called Moses to go free His people from slavery, Moses began looking to his deficiencies and what disqualified him for the task God set before him. He looked at his weakness more than he looked to the strength and power of God. Take a moment to reflect on this. Has God called you to something you felt you didn't have the capacity to do? What has kept you from moving forward? Be encouraged today that if God has called you to it, He will equip you for it. He is not looking for the most qualified; He wants to do wonders through those who will obey Him despite the odds.

_____

_____

_____

_____

_____

God, teach me to move forward, looking to You,
leaning on Your strength, and not being
stopped by my weaknesses. Amen.

PERFECT PROCESS

May he work perfection into every part of you giving you all that you need to fulfill your destiny. And may he express through you all that is excellent and pleasing to him through your life-union with Jesus the Anointed One who is to receive all glory forever! Amen!

—HEBREWS 13:21 TPT

The process of realizing your purpose may feel as though you are walking through fire, but God is just refining and preparing you for the good works He has set apart for you. You don't have to worry about being perfect or already prepared, because God Himself, the designer of your destiny, will lovingly walk with you and will work perfection into you. God Himself will equip you. Ask God to prepare you and show you your destiny. Have you taken notice of any areas in your life that can hinder you from moving forward and need work?

_____

_____

_____

_____

Father God, complete Your work in me. Take me through whatever process necessary. As long as You are walking through it with me, I know I will be okay. Amen.

MADE STRONG

So be made strong even in your weakness by lifting up your tired hands in prayer and worship. And strengthen your weak knees, for as you keep walking forward on God's paths all your stumbling ways will be divinely healed!

—HEBREWS 12:12–13 TPT

While we may run away and hide behind weaknesses, God confronts and uncovers them to bring His strength over them! Don't allow weakness to discourage you from moving forward; instead, seek God through prayer and worship. You will see that everything that was once an obstacle will bow before Him and melt away, as you are in His presence. Remember, you are more than a conqueror through Jesus! Think about your weaknesses; do they ever keep you from seeking God?

_____

_____

_____

_____

Father God, You are my strength, so I refuse to give my weaknesses power any longer. They have to bow before You! In Jesus' name, amen.

COME WORSHIP

The eyes of the Lord are upon even the weakest worshipers who love him—those who wait in hope and expectation for the strong, steady love of God.

—PSALM 33:18 TPT

What is your response when you are feeling at your weakest and lowest? Do you hide from God or do you run to Him? I want you to know that God is not afraid of the messy feelings, confusion, or struggles you are facing that are causing you to feel powerless. He wants to interrupt all of that to uplift you, breathe hope back into you, and heal you. If this is where you have been, there is an open invitation to come into His presence—weaknesses and all—to worship Him, and He will come and rest on you.

_____

_____

_____

_____

_____

_____

Father God, everything melts away when I am with You, so draw closer and nearer; my soul longs for Your presence. Amen.

CONSTANT PRAISE

Bring your constant praise to God the Father because of what Christ has done for you!

—COLOSSIANS 3:17 TPT

Don't allow anything to stop your praise. Disappointment can come and trouble can rise, but let your praise continue. In your triumphs and successes, remember that every good and perfect gift comes from Him, so give Him due praise. In the highs, lows, and the in-between, remember that He is always worthy and good. No matter what your season is right now, be constant in your praise and let Him fill you with joy. Take this space to praise and thank Him for all that He has done.

_____

_____

_____

_____

_____

_____

_____

Father God, I praise You for Your marvelous works and the never-ending love You have given me. Thank You for all that You have done and all that You do. Amen.

PRINCE OF PEACE

"And everything I've taught you is so that the peace which is in me will be in you and will give you great confidence as you rest in me. For in this unbelieving world you will experience trouble and sorrows, but you must be courageous, for I have conquered the world!"

—JOHN 16:33 TPT

We were never meant to find lasting peace here on Earth. Jesus is the Prince of Peace and He desires to give you everlasting peace. His words will bring you the courage and assurance you need. When all you see around you is chaos and thoughts are running rampant in your mind, draw near to the one who can calm the storm with just a word. Take time to reflect on who or what you run to for security and peace. Is Jesus your source?

_____

_____

_____

_____

_____

_____

Father God, remind me that You are my source of peace; teach me to look to You and to listen for Your words. Amen.

REST AND TRUST

"Come to me, all who labor and are heavy laden, and I will give you rest. Take my yoke upon you, and learn from me, for I am gentle and lowly in heart, and you will find rest for your souls. For my yoke is easy, and my burden is light."

—MATTHEW 11:28–30 ESV

Resting in God signifies that you are trusting in God. You may not have all the answers, and that is okay, because you take comfort that God has the answers and He is sovereign in all of His ways. God has your life in His hands. If you are tired and weary, then come to Him and allow Him to give you the rest that your soul is in need of. Are you trusting that God has your situation taken care of? Surrender yourself and your cares in His presence.

_____

_____

_____

_____

_____

_____

Father God, would You come and overwhelm what is overwhelming me? Meet me with rest and give me peace that can come only from You. Amen.

GOD IS ON YOUR SIDE

The very moment I call to you for a father's help the tide of battle turns and my enemies flee. This one thing I know: God is on my side! I trust in the Lord. And I praise him!

—PSALM 56:9–10 TPT

No matter who or what you are up against, in this you can trust: God is on your side, and He is not in the business of losing. Give your battle to God and allow your Father to fight for, defend, and protect you. You don't have to face this alone; He is your help in the day of trouble. What battle are you facing? Can you trust God with it?

_____

_____

_____

_____

_____

_____

_____

Father God, I hand over this battle to You and I declare that You have won it! There is victory in Jesus' name. Amen.

GOD MY HEALER

He heals the brokenhearted and binds up their wounds.

—PSALM 147:3 NIV

God feels your pain. He has heard your cry, and not one tear has gone unseen by Him. He desires to be your healer and to pick up the pieces that have been scattered. Where there used to be brokenness, God wants you to see break-through. Where there was a troubled spirit, He will cause beauty to rise from the ashes and testimony to be birthed. Allow God into your hurt and don't bury it away any longer; it is time to allow His healing to come. Is there any part of you that needs healing? Let God know.

_____

_____

_____

_____

_____

_____

_____

Father God, You are my rescuer and healer. I know
You are for me, so come and help me in my pain and
remove anything that is not of You. Amen.

AT THE END OF IT ALL

Yahweh, you alone are my inheritance. You are my prize, my pleasure, and my portion. You hold my destiny and its timing in your hands.

—PSALM 16:5 TPT

A week before my aunt passed away after a 10-year battle with cancer, I received a call from her. She said, "Write this down and never forget it. At the end of it all, the only thing that matters is that I followed Jesus." To this day, I never forget the sound of her voice saying this, and I have prayed that God would direct my heart to live this way. He is all that you will ever need; He is the treasure we lay a hold of, and He is the satisfaction of our souls. In all the searching and wandering we can do, the answer to finding this eternal fulfilment is Jesus. Take time to reflect on what you turn to for fulfilment. Where have you been trying to find it?

_____

_____

_____

_____

_____

_____

*God, teach me to love You in this way; may
You be the treasure of my soul. Amen.*

*Now is the time to know that
God is able. To connect your current
reality with God's present ability.*

—PRISCILLA SHIRER

A FINAL WORD

What an amazing journey we have been on together. I want to congratulate you for finishing this journal and being willing to do the real work!

You set aside the necessary time, allowed God to minister to your heart through His Word, and opened up to reflection and to asking yourself the tougher questions. God will honor this time that you have given Him, and I know that even now you are beginning to see the fruits come forth. I am beyond excited for you because it is just the beginning.

It has been a great privilege to dive into the Bible with you. As you come to the end of this journal, I want you to remember that uncovering the Word of God is discovering treasure. This treasure is far more precious than gold and silver. This treasure will open your heart and mind to see the beauty of the Lord and give you the wisdom to understand the amazing purposes He has for you.

I pray that this journal is just the beginning and that it has served as a catalyst for what is to come. I hope that it has stirred something deep within you. I pray that you recognize that yearning God has placed in you for more of Him. I pray that Psalm 119 comes alive in you and the Word of God becomes the hope of you heart and desire of your soul.

Remember, there is so much more that God wants to show you, and all you have to do is call out to Him and He will answer—ask and it will be given to you, seek and you will find. No matter what may come, anchor yourself in the truth of the Word and you will see the mighty hand of God in your life!

ACKNOWLEDGMENTS

TO MY MOM AND DAD, you taught me the power of prayer and have been the evidence of it. Thank you both for showing me that battles are won through prayer. Your life has been a testimony of Matthew 7:7-8, and because of you I believe that too. I love you both and I am proud to be your daughter. Junior, Jessi, and Josh, thank you for being rocks in my life—you have protected, covered, and loved me. Monica and Melissa, thank you for your support. Maddy, Matthew, and Darla, this is for you. I pray that you grow up knowing you have been set apart by God. Tia Erika, Kevin, and Sofia, here is my promise I made, and that God fulfilled. Tia, you marked my life with your faith, N.E.D. Tiffany, my covenant friend, you have been with me every step of the way. Thank you for being a fulfillment of Proverbs 27:9 for me. To my Joni and Friends Family, especially Laura, Pastor Billy, and Joni, thank you for taking time to teach and mold me into who I am today. To the Jesus Clubs, and to every student I have met, I thought of you as I wrote this book. My heart is always with you.

ABOUT THE AUTHOR

AMY AYALA is a digital missionary whose passion is spreading the Word of God through social media platforms. Serving four years as a public high school campus missionary taught her the heart of God is meeting people where they are at. God has been leading Amy to share the Bible on social media platforms like TikTok, Instagram, and YouTube. Follow her on all three platforms @amylynnettee.